British Foreign

D0808752

1919–39

THIRD EDITION

Alan Farmer

Waltham Forest Publi

The Publishers would like to thank the following for permission to reproduce copyright illustrations: © Bettmann/CORBIS, pages 46, 74, 114; © CORBIS, page 42; Getty Images, page 83; © Hulton-Deutsch Collection/CORBIS, pages 18, 98, 116, 140; Reproduced with permission of Punch, Ltd. www.punch.co.uk, pages 44, 81, 115, 138; Solo Syndication/Associated Newspapers, pages 50, 76, 121, 146; © Underwood & Underwood/CORBIS, page 21.

The Publishers would also like to thank the following for permission to reproduce copyright material: Oxford, Cambridge and RSA (OCR) examinations for extracts used on pages 125, 159.

Every effort has been made to trace all copyright holders, but if any have been inadvertently overlooked the Publishers will be pleased to make the necessary arrangements at the first opportunity.

Although every effort has been made to ensure that website addresses are correct at time of going to press, Hodder Murray cannot be held responsible for the content of any website mentioned in this book. It is sometimes possible to find a relocated web page by typing in the address of the home page for a website in the URL window of your browser.

Orders: please contact Bookpoint Ltd, 130 Milton Park, Abingdon, Oxon OX14 4SB. Telephone: (44) 01235 827720. Fax: (44) 01235 400454. Lines are open 9.00–6.00, Monday to Saturday, with a 24-hour message answering service. Visit our website at www.hoddereducation.co.uk

© Alan Farmer 2006

First published in 2006 by
Hodder Murray, an imprint of Hodder Education,
a member of the Hodder Headline Group
338 Euston Road
London NW1 3BH

Impression number   10 9 8 7 6 5 4 3 2 1
Year   2010 2009 2008 2007 2006

Cover photo shows [to follow]
Typeset in Baskerville 10/12pt and produced by Gray Publishing, Tunbridge Wells
Printed in Malta

A catalogue record for this title is available from the British Library

ISBN-10: 0 340 90703 7
ISBN-13: 978 0 340 90703 0

Contents

Chapter 6 The Coming of War 1939

Chapter 7 Interpreting British Foreign Policy 1919–39

Glossary

Index

Dedication

Keith Randell (1943–2002)

The *Access to History* series was conceived and developed by Keith, who created a series to 'cater for students as they are, not as we might wish them to be'. He leaves a living legacy of a series that for over 20 years has provided a trusted, stimulating and well-loved accompaniment to post-16 study. Our aim with these new editions is to continue to offer students the best possible support for their studies.

1 The Making of British Foreign Policy

POINTS TO CONSIDER
This introductory chapter aims to provide you with a framework for understanding the making of British foreign policy in the inter-war years (1918–39). It will do this by considering the following questions:

- What was Britain's position in 1918–19? To what extent had the First World War diminished its power?
- What problems did British statesmen face in the inter-war years?
- Who made British foreign policy?
- What were Britain's main interests in foreign policy?

Key dates
1918   End of the First World War
1919   Treaty of Versailles
1939   Start of the Second World War

Key question
How great was Britain in 1919?

Key date
End of the First World War: November 1918

Key terms
Armistice
A truce: the suspension of hostilities.

RAF
The Royal Air Force, formed in April 1918, was the youngest of Britain's armed services.

1 | Britain's Position in 1919

In November 1918, after four years of savage conflict, an **armistice** finally brought the First World War – or Great War – to an end. In Britain, as in other victorious countries, there was great rejoicing and hope of a golden era of peace and prosperity. David Lloyd George, the Prime Minister, talked of Britain becoming a 'land fit for heroes'.

Britain seemed to have emerged from the First World War in an immensely strong position. Unlike much of Belgium and northern France, it had escaped devastation. Britain had lost only five per cent of its active male population, whereas France had lost 10 per cent and Germany 15 per cent. In 1918 Britain's mobilisation of military resources was at its peak. Britain ended the war with:

- an army of 5,500,000 men
- the Royal Navy having 58 battleships, with over 100 cruisers, and a host of lesser craft
- the **RAF** having over 20,000 planes.

The British Empire, which amounted to nearly a quarter of the world's land surface, had greatly assisted the mother country's war effort, providing essential raw materials and some 2,500,000 'colonial' troops. The war seemed to provide proof of the Empire's unity and utility.

The weakness of Britain's enemies

Britain's strong position in 1918 was enhanced by the weakness of its traditional rivals. Germany, the main threat to Britain before 1914, was defeated; its army had ceased to exist as a major fighting force; its fleet was in the hands of the British; its empire was lost; and its economy seemed near collapse.

Russia, Britain's ally in the First World War but a rival for much of the nineteenth century, was in chaos. A Bolshevik government, led by Lenin, had seized power in November 1917 but was now under attack from 'White' Russian forces, backed by various Allied powers, including Britain. The Russian economy was in tatters and several provinces had taken advantage of the turmoil to declare their independence from Russia.

The lack of major rivals

Britain seemed to have little to fear from the other great powers that had emerged victorious from the war. France had been hard hit by the conflict. Although the USA and Japan were much stronger than they had been in 1914, neither seemed likely to pose an immediate challenge. The USA had aligned itself decisively with Britain in the war and common ties of language, culture and tradition meant that there was already talk of a 'special relationship' between the two Anglo-Saxon powers. Britain was also on good terms with Japan. The two countries had been allied since 1902 and the alliance had held throughout the war.

Britain's economic strength

The First World War had less economic impact on Britain than many had feared. Britain's enormous reserves of wealth and its established hold on many overseas markets cushioned the blow. There was no great trade deficit; indeed Britain's **balance of payments** remained in the black for the war years as a whole. The elimination of German competition helped British manufacturers. The great industrial effort of the war appeared to have demonstrated the strength and flexibility of the British economy. In spite of millions of men being mobilised for the armed forces, industrial output had hardly fallen. So healthy was the economy that Britain had been able to pay for the war largely out of its own resources and had even been able to loan vast sums of money to other Allied governments, especially Russia. Although Britain did owe money to the USA, most of this debt had been contracted by Britain on behalf of its allies, who owed Britain far more money than it owed the USA.

Balance of payments
The difference between a nation's total receipts (in all forms) from foreign countries and its total payments to foreign countries.

Key term

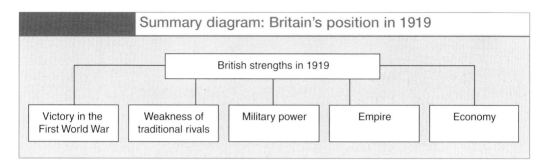

Summary diagram: Britain's position in 1919

British strengths in 1919

| Victory in the First World War | Weakness of traditional rivals | Military power | Empire | Economy |

Key question
What were the main problems facing Britain after 1918?

2 | Problems Facing British Statesmen

Britain's position in world affairs, however, was not as strong as at first appeared. Consequently, British statesmen after 1918 faced serious problems as they struggled to preserve both peace and Britain's status.

The threat from Germany and the USA pre-1914

Britain's influential position in world affairs in the nineteenth century was due to a number of inter-related factors. The **Industrial Revolution** that started in Britain had ensured that it was both the **workshop of the world** and **banking house of the world** before 1870. Throughout the eighteenth and nineteenth centuries the Royal Navy had ruled the waves, ensuring that Britain was secure from attack. Economic and naval supremacy had helped Britain to acquire the most extensive empire the world had ever seen (see Figure 1.1).

However, by 1900 Britain's economic position was threatened by Germany and the USA, which had become serious industrial rivals. By the early years of the twentieth century Germany even posed a potential military threat.

Economic problems after 1918

By 1919 Germany had been defeated. However, the First World War, far from boosting Britain's economic position, had imposed serious strain. The financial costs had been massive – £7 million a day, only paid for by heavy borrowing. The war resulted in an 11-fold increase in the **national debt**, the annual interest payments of which consumed a large percentage of central government expenditure in the inter-war years. Moreover Britain had been forced to sell off some of its overseas investments, which had a damaging effect on the country's balance of payments. To make matters worse, the war had damaged Britain's industrial capacity. In many cases normal replacement and improvement of industrial plant and machinery had been postponed, as Britain struggled to produce the military materials needed to wage war against Germany. Britain had also lost many lucrative markets, especially in Latin America and the Far East, to the USA and Japan. As a consequence, the British economy stuttered through the inter-war years. Even in the 1920s British manufacturers had

Key terms

Industrial Revolution
The economic and social changes arising out of the replacement of home-based work with manufacturing in factories with power-driven machinery.

Workshop of the world
Britain had produced most of the world's industrial goods before 1870.

Banking house of the world
Britain had surplus capital (money) to invest in projects around the world in the nineteenth century.

National debt
Money borrowed by a government and not yet repaid.

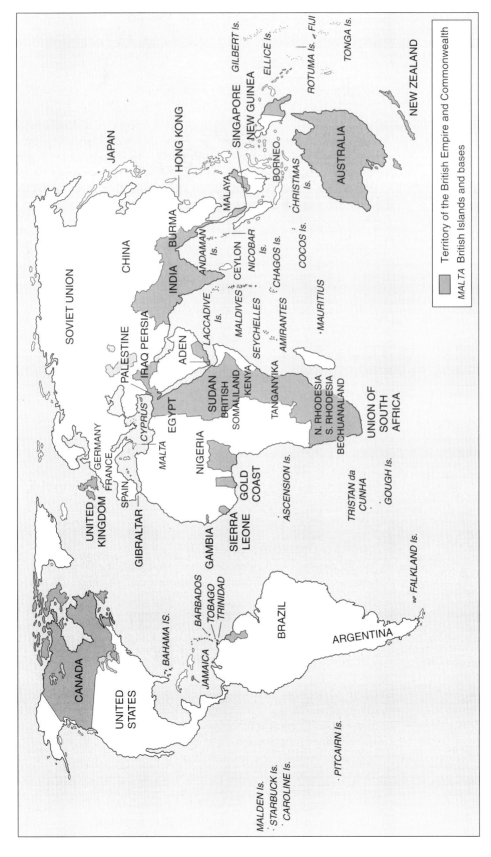

Figure 1.1: British Empire after 1918.

a poor export record and there was a high rate of unemployment. The world-wide depression of the 1930s further rocked the economy (see pages 66). Britain's share of world trade thus steadily declined after 1918.

Defence problems

Unlike the USA, Britain could not ignore developments in Europe. Moreover, Britain was also a great imperial power with global commitments. Many politicians on both the **right** and the **left** saw Britain as the policeman of the world. Those on the right believed Britain could and should maintain British interests wherever and whenever they were challenged. Those on the left thought Britain should enforce the decisions of the **League of Nations** (see pages 53–5). Indeed at no time in the inter-war years could British ministers free themselves from the popular assumption that on them rested the responsibility for defending the victims of aggression in any part of the world.

The economic and financial weakness meant there was a growing disparity between Britain's global commitments and its capacity to meet them. British military spending was massively reduced in the 1920s and early 1930s. In 1913 30 per cent of Britain's government expenditure had been on defence. By 1933 this had fallen to 10 per cent. By the 1930s the fleet was growing old, the army was under 400,000 strong and the RAF was only the fifth largest in the world. By 1935 only one major arms' manufacturer (Vickers-Armstrong) was still in business.

Lack of allies

Britain could not rely on others to help in its police-keeping role. The First World War alliance with France soon wore thin. In 1921 the British Foreign Secretary, Lord Curzon, wrote that 'in almost every quarter of the globe … the representatives of France are actively pursuing a policy which is either unfriendly to British interests or, if not that, is consecrated to the promotion of a French interest which is inconsistent with ours'. Indeed in some quarters there was a fear of an over-strong France that might pursue **Napoleonic dreams of empire**.

The USA emerged from the First World War as potentially the world's greatest power. Without US financial, economic and ultimately military help it is unlikely that Britain and France would have won the war. But after 1919 the USA was reluctant to involve itself in international affairs, especially in the 1930s when its assistance was most needed. Most US presidents were not indifferent to Europe (and Asia), but their willingness and ability to exert themselves was severely constrained by US public opinion, which was strongly **isolationist**. While many British politicians hoped for a closer co-operation with the USA, British governments soon recognised that they could not base their foreign policy on it. In 1932 the Prime Minister, Stanley Baldwin, said 'You will get nothing from America but words: big words but only words'.

Key terms

Right
Those who are inclined towards conservatism or who are strongly nationalist.

Left
Those who want to change society and who might incline towards socialism or communism.

League of Nations
A global organisation set up in 1919 to resolve international disputes and to maintain the 1919 peace settlement.

Napoleonic dreams of empire
In the early nineteenth century the French Emperor Napoleon Bonaparte had conquered most of Europe.

Isolationist
One who supports avoiding political entanglements with other countries.

Imperial weakness

Nor could Britain depend on its empire, which was not as strong as it seemed. There were growing **nationalist** movements in many parts of it, especially in India, the '**jewel in the crown**'. Even the **Dominions** – especially South Africa, Canada and (after 1922) the Irish Free State – were anxious to achieve greater autonomy and to develop their own separate foreign policies, rather than be committed, even with prior consultation, to the consequences of British diplomacy.

The foreign threat

British statesmen had to face the fact that several potentially very strong nations had grievances and ambitions that might well threaten world peace and even Britain's security. Germany, Russia, Italy and Japan, for a variety of reasons, were dissatisfied with both the peace settlement of 1919 (see pages 22–31) and the status quo.

The threat, or perhaps more accurately the perceived threat, from these countries varied considerably in terms of time and scale:

- Russia was seen as a threat in the early 1920s.
- Italy was regarded as a nuisance in the early 1920s and as a more serious threat after 1935.
- Japan was on good terms with Britain until the early 1930s. By the late 1930s, however, it was a potential opponent.
- Germany did not become a serious threat until after 1935. By the late 1930s, it was seen as posing the greatest threat to Britain.

Key terms

Nationalist
Favouring or striving for the unity, independence or interests of a nation.

Jewel in the crown
India was the most highly prized part of the British Empire. It had a huge population and thus tremendous trading potential.

Dominions
Countries within the British Empire that had considerable – in some cases almost total – self-rule. They did not necessarily take orders from Britain.

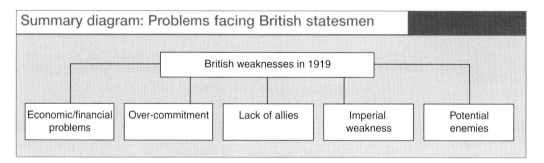

Summary diagram: Problems facing British statesmen

British weaknesses in 1919

Economic/financial problems | Over-commitment | Lack of allies | Imperial weakness | Potential enemies

3 | Who Made British Foreign Policy?

Prime Ministers and Foreign Secretaries

The central column of policy-making machinery extended down from the prime minister, through the **Cabinet** and Foreign Office to British diplomatic missions around the world. The relationship between Prime Minister and Foreign Secretary was crucial. Stanley Baldwin delegated a great deal of responsibility to his Foreign Secretaries (especially Austen Chamberlain). At the other extreme, Neville Chamberlain and Ramsay MacDonald, like Lloyd George before them, tried to run their own foreign policies and, as a result, sometimes came into conflict with their Foreign Secretaries. Chamberlain, for example, found himself at odds

Key question
Who had most control over British foreign policy: Prime Ministers or Foreign Secretaries?

Key term

Cabinet
Senior ministers of the British government who meet regularly to discuss policy.

with Anthony Eden in 1937–8 (see page 103). Usually, however, Prime Ministers chose Foreign Secretaries who they could trust and to whom they felt able to hand over substantial authority.

Table 1.1: British governments, Prime Ministers and Foreign Secretaries 1919–39

Governments	Prime Ministers	Foreign Secretaries
War Cabinet Dec. 1916–Jan. 1919	D. Lloyd George	A.J. Balfour
Coalition Jan. 1919–Oct. 1922	D. Lloyd George	A.J. Balfour (until Oct. 1919) then Lord Curzon
Conservative Oct. 1922–May 1923	A. Bonar Law	Lord Curzon
Conservative May 1923–Jan. 1924	Stanley Baldwin	Lord Curzon
Labour Jan. 1924–Nov. 1924	Ramsay MacDonald	Ramsay MacDonald
Conservative Nov. 1924–June 1929	Stanley Baldwin	Austen Chamberlain
Labour June 1929–Aug. 1931	Ramsay MacDonald	Arthur Henderson
National Aug. 1931–June 1935	Ramsay MacDonald	Marquess of Reading then Sir John Simson
National (Conservative) June 1935–May 1937	Stanley Baldwin	Sir Samuel Hoare then Sir Anthony Eden
National (Conservative) May 1937–May 1940	Neville Chamberlain	Anthony Eden then Lord Halifax

The British Cabinet

Key question
How important was the Cabinet in determining British foreign policy?

Prime Ministers (and their Foreign Secretaries) undoubtedly made important decisions. However, the shaping of British foreign policy did not totally depend on their actions. All Prime Ministers and Foreign Secretaries had to consider the views of other members of the Cabinet. It is true that most of the time the Cabinet as a whole had relatively little say on foreign policy matters, if only because few diplomatic issues actually reached Cabinet level. (The Cabinet had so many other important domestic matters to discuss.) However, all Prime Ministers realised the necessity of having the support of most of the Cabinet, particularly on key foreign issues. Even Neville Chamberlain, who very much conducted his own foreign policy, frequently heeded the advice of his Cabinet – sometimes against his better judgement. Members of all governments saw themselves as a team, and unity was a foremost consideration. When real disagreement was evident, there were invariably attempts to build a consensus and to reconcile divisions.

The role of Parliament

The Cabinet was ultimately responsible to Parliament. Although Parliament rarely intervened in day-to-day foreign affairs, many individual Members of Parliament (MPs) (such as Winston Churchill) were very interested in foreign policy developments and often questioned the wisdom of government policy. In the last resort Parliament could force governments to take particular courses of action. For example, given the feeling in the House of Commons, Chamberlain would have found it very difficult not to have declared war on Germany on 3 September 1939 (see page 149).

Key question
How important was Parliament in determining British foreign policy?

British public opinion

Parliament, in turn, represented public opinion. After 1918 British statesmen no longer had quite the same room for manoeuvre in foreign affairs as their counterparts in earlier generations. The 1918 general election in Britain was the first to be conducted on the basis of full **manhood suffrage** and there was also a limited **franchise for women**. (The franchise was finally extended to women on the same terms as men in 1928.) Politicians could now gain and preserve power only by winning the support of a far larger electorate than in the past. In consequence, public opinion had a far greater influence on foreign policy than ever before.

While the public as a whole rarely was interested in the details of foreign policy, public opinion did set the broad ideological framework within which foreign policy operated. Most people in Britain in the inter-war years, for example, preferred governments to spend money on health, social services and education rather than on armaments and adventures abroad. In the early 1930s successive British governments had to be seen to be supporting the League of Nations and the idea of collective security, both popular with the electorate (see pages 53–7). Throughout most of the inter-war years British governments could not ignore the deep-seated yearning for peace on the part of the electorate. Ironically, in 1939 Chamberlain may have been persuaded to take a tougher line against Hitler by the pressure of public opinion. He could certainly not have risked going to war in 1939 without being sure he had the firm support of the majority of the country.

Key question
How important was public opinion in determining British foreign policy?

Manhood suffrage
The right of all men to vote.

Franchise for women
The right of women to vote.

Key terms

The mass media

The public, in turn, were influenced by the mass media, particularly by the press but increasingly in the 1930s by radio and **newsreels** which people saw when they went to the cinema. (Television was only introduced in the mid-1930s and only a very small percentage of the population could afford a television set.) The extent to which the media were influenced by – or influenced – both the government and public opinion is keenly debated by historians and social scientists in general. The various media were certainly in a position to shape the agenda of public debate by focusing on certain news items and giving them particular

Key question
What impact did the mass media have on determining British foreign policy?

Newsreels
Short news programmes shown between feature films at cinemas.

Key term

colouring and significance. In the 1930s, for example, newsreels invariably showed ranks of marching soldiers when reporting on Nazi Germany. This may well have given British people the impression that Nazi Germany was a more militarised state than was perhaps the case.

Developments in communications meant that statesmen now negotiated in the full glare of publicity. Day-to-day dealings with foreign countries were subject to much greater scrutiny, sometimes with disastrous effects on difficult and delicate negotiations; for example, the Hoare–Laval Pact in 1935 (see pages 83–4).

The press

By 1937 there were over 1500 newspapers and more than 3000 **periodicals**. Virtually every family took a national newspaper and most local newspapers enjoyed a good circulation. The press provided a wide range of views. *The Times*, although not the most widely read, remained the most influential paper: it was viewed abroad as the voice of the British government and its editor was regarded as one of the four most powerful figures in Britain (along with the King, Prime Minister and Archbishop of Canterbury). *The Times* prided itself on the breadth and depth of its foreign coverage and employed a vast team of well-informed foreign correspondents. The *Daily Express*, owned by Lord Beaverbrook, claimed the world's largest daily circulation (2–3 million). A radical, right-wing paper, it was popular with most income groups. It faced competition from Lord Rothmere's *Daily Mail*. The *Daily Telegraph*, another pro-Conservative newspaper, also had a rising circulation. The *News Chronicle*, a Liberal paper, sold over a million copies daily. The *Daily Herald* was the only major daily paper consistently to support the Labour Party in the 1930s. Press freedom ensured that there was always critical comment of government actions from one paper or another.

Radio's influence

By the late 1930s some nine million homes owned a radio. Controlled by the British Broadcasting Corporation (BBC), radio was heavily regulated by the British government. Sir John Reith, the BBC's Director-General, aware that the BBC was perceived abroad as the mouthpiece of the government, operated with great caution. Thus, BBC coverage of international events hardly ever offered critical comment and opponents of government action were given little opportunity to air their views.

Cinema's influence

In the mid-1930s there were over 4300 cinemas in Britain and some 23 million people went to the cinema at least once a week. Cinemas showed newsreels between the main feature and the **B featured film**. The newsreels were produced by five companies: three British and two US owned. Virtually all the companies provided a highly sanitised view of foreign policy (if they

Key term

Periodicals
Journals or magazines that are usually published weekly or monthly.

Key term

B featured film
In the early twentieth century, cinema-goers usually watched two films: the main feature and a subsidiary film, which was usually shorter, cheaper to make and had secondary billing.

provided anything at all). In the autumn of 1938, for example, Neville Chamberlain, on his return from the Munich Conference (see pages 115–16), was presented as a successful peacemaker, whose actions were supported by a relieved British public. This was a somewhat simplistic, but not necessarily false, interpretation of events.

The Civil Service

It is possible to argue that foreign policy-making was as much in the hands of professional career civil servants in the Foreign Office as politicians. Robert Vansittart, Permanent Under-Secretary of State in the Foreign Office 1930–8, was certainly able to exert considerable control over foreign policy.

Key question
To what extent was foreign policy determined by the British Civil Service?

Other Whitehall departments – the India Office, the Colonial Office, the Dominion Office (set up in 1925), the War Office, the Admiralty and the Air Ministry – also influenced foreign policy-making. Treasury officials, because they were in a position to scrutinise any proposal involving government spending, also had considerable authority. Therefore foreign policy-making was handled by a plethora of rival Civil Service departments, each with its own specialists, who remained at their post whatever party was in office. Some historians think that the existence of this entrenched bureaucracy resulted in continuity, compromise and lower common-denominator policies which satisfied most interests to some degree but may have prevented radical changes of policy.

Many of the senior civil servants came from similar backgrounds to the politicians. They attended the same public schools (especially Eton and Harrow) and the same universities (overwhelmingly Oxford and Cambridge), and often frequented the same London clubs. Some historians think that this 'élite' controlled foreign policy in their own 'class' interests. This conclusion, which does not account for the fact that many of the so-called élite had very different views on many foreign policy issues, is far too sweeping.

Foreign influence

The final – and obvious – point is that British foreign policy was largely shaped and determined by the actions of non-Britons. British prime ministers, foreign secretaries, cabinets, parliaments, public opinion, media or civil servants had limited control over the policies of Hitler, Stalin, Mussolini or the **Japanese militarists**. In fact, Britain could not even exert much influence over the policies of more friendly governments, such as those of France and the USA. British foreign policy-makers had to respond to the real (and potential) actions of a variety of powers, both friendly and hostile.

Japanese militarists
In the 1930s Japan was controlled by military-dominated governments who wanted to expand Japan's empire.

Key term

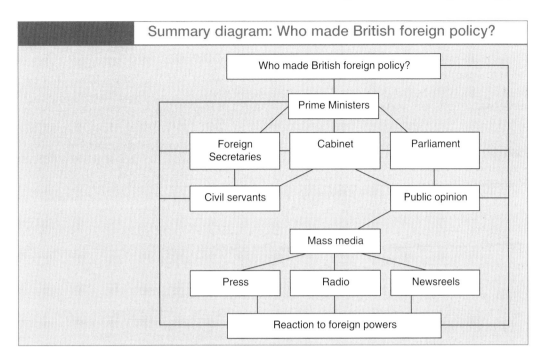

Summary diagram: Who made British foreign policy?

Who made British foreign policy?

Prime Ministers

Foreign Secretaries · Cabinet · Parliament

Civil servants · Public opinion

Mass media

Press · Radio · Newsreels

Reaction to foreign powers

4 | British Interests

Political differences

British statesmen responded to the difficulties they faced in different ways. Ministers in Labour governments, for example, were more prepared to come to terms with the **USSR** and professed a greater faith in disarmament and the League of Nations than did Conservative ministers. The Conservative Party, in power for most of the period 1919–39, was never fully united on foreign or imperial affairs. Some Conservative MPs, like Winston Churchill, favoured Britain taking a firm stand against Hitler's Germany. Others supported the policy of appeasing Hitler.

Nevertheless, while there were differences of emphasis, most governments, whether Conservative or Labour, tended to adopt similar policies throughout the inter-war period. In part, this reflected the general political situation. On the two occasions when the Labour Party was in power (1924 and 1929–31) it depended on Liberal support and was more moderate than would have been suggested by the tone of Labour MPs' speeches when in opposition.

Although there were divisions in the Conservative Party, an overwhelming majority of its MPs supported the policies of Stanley Baldwin and Neville Chamberlain, rather than those of Winston Churchill, who was out of office for most of the 1930s.

Given the fact that many people continued to vote Liberal, both the Conservative and Labour Parties tended to appeal to the middle ground, with the result that there was **consensus politics**. This was particularly true in the 1930s, when **National Governments** were in power.

Throughout this period there was also strong continuity in Foreign Office personnel. Their experience and expertise gave the officials considerable influence over most Prime Ministers and Foreign Secretaries. This helped to ensure continuity in style and purpose. Prudence, pragmatism, moderation, a tendency to understatement and irony; all tended to be features of the British government's style, almost regardless of which party was in power.

British concerns

Preserving peace

A secret Foreign Office memorandum in April 1926 described Britain's main concerns:

> We have got all that we want – perhaps more. Our sole object is to keep what we have and live in peace. … To the casual observer our foreign policy may appear to lack consistency and continuity, but both are there. We keep our hands free in order to throw our weight into the scale and on behalf of peace. The maintenance of the balance of power and the preservation of the status quo have been our guiding lights for many decades and will so continue.

Peace seemed the greatest of national interests. The scale of the bloodshed in the Great War made both politicians and public recoil from the prospect of a new war. For most of the inter-war period (until 1939) no electoral advantage could be gained by waving the flag and beating the drum. Peace helped to promote commerce, essential to British prosperity. There was also an awareness that Britain was increasingly vulnerable. Submarines could threaten the navy, so long the shield of Britain, while aircraft could attack British cities, however strong the navy. Britain seemed to have everything to lose and nothing to gain from a major war.

Preserving the balance of power

Most British governments wished to maintain the **balance of power** in Europe as the best insurance against the renewal of war. But most were also reluctant to assume any definite commitments to further this aim. Many Britons believed the First World War had been caused by a rigid **alliance system** and fixed military plans. As a result, most British governments had no intention of binding the country to preserve the status quo; in particular, the new, questionable boundaries of eastern Europe. This was to remain a cardinal tenet of British policy until 1939.

World power

Most politicians appreciated the importance of Europe to Britain, but very few considered Britain a fully fledged European state. British interests were global rather than just continental. It was thought that the preservation of the Empire was essential if Britain was to remain a great world power. Although politicians claimed that self-government was the ultimate destiny of every

Key term

National Governments Governments that were dominated by the Conservatives but which were supported by some Labour and Liberal MPs.

Key terms

Balance of power British governments had long tried to ensure that no nation was so strong that it could dominate Europe and become a potential threat to Britain.

Alliance system Before 1914 Europe had been divided into two armed camps: the Triple Entente (Britain, France and Russia) against the Triple Alliance (Germany, Austria–Hungary and Italy).

part of the British Empire, most were determined to preserve the imperial union in some form.

The importance of the USA

Another key British aim was to remain on good terms with the USA. Britain, as all governments realised, could not afford even a minor quarrel with America. The USA was already a great economic power and was also potentially a great military power. Britain might well need its assistance in the future, just as it had in the First World War. A permanent quarrel with America was unthinkable.

The defence of Britain

A vital concern of all governments was to ensure that Britain was adequately defended. Defence policy was based on four main objectives:

- the security of the United Kingdom
- the protection of essential British trade routes
- defence of the Empire
- a readiness to co-operate in the defence of Britain's allies.

Throughout the period, British governments had to assess Britain's defence requirements in the light of the current international situation and in terms of what the country could afford. Successive governments – Conservative and Labour – decided that the country could afford very little. In 1920 £519 million was spent on defence; in 1929 only £123 million.

In July 1919 Lloyd George's government decided, and the armed forces planned on the assumption, that 'the British Empire will not be involved in any large war over the next ten years'. This 'Ten Year Rule', which was used to justify keeping defence spending as low as possible, was to continue until 1932. It made some sense: Britain faced severe social and economic problems and there was no serious threat to world peace in the 1920s. However, savage defence cuts had unfortunate consequences for Britain's domestic arms industry, which virtually disappeared. There was no guarantee, therefore, that Britain would have the industrial capability or the time to re-arm if a serious enemy appeared.

The British army

After 1919 Britain's army was cut massively. It rapidly reverted to its pre-war role of imperial police force. Lacking the traditional esteem of the Royal Navy or the novelty appeal of the RAF, the army was the 'Cinderella' service. It was always short of men (despite high unemployment) and increasingly dependent on obsolete weapons and equipment.

The Royal Navy

The Royal Navy, although treated less harshly, also suffered. Agreements with Britain's naval competitors (see pages 56–7) ensured that there were no replacement battleships. Cruisers and destroyers were steadily reduced. Naval stores were run down and Britain's string of bases throughout the world was neglected, with the exception of Singapore.

The RAF

The RAF preserved its separate identity but remained small in size. However, there was a growing belief in the effect of the **bomber deterrent**. Many people thought that planes were the cheapest way of preventing future aggression or of winning a war if one came.

Appeasement

Most British politicians hoped that sensible policies of compromise, conciliation and concession would prevent conflict. Such policies were later called appeasement. The meaning of the word has been so stretched and distorted since 1939 that some historians believe the word should no longer be used. Appeasement can be used to cover all aspects of British diplomacy between the two world wars. Or it can be used more specifically to describe Neville Chamberlain's policies towards Germany in 1937 and 1938 (see pages 97–9).

Since the Second World War appeasement has tended to have a derogatory meaning, and the word is often used to mean a craven surrender to force. But for most of the inter-war years, appeasement was seen as a positive concept: the continuation of a long British diplomatic tradition of trying to settle disputes peacefully. Those who opposed appeasement were seen as cranks or war-mongers. Only the failure of Neville Chamberlain's policies in 1938–9 (when he actually abandoned appeasement!) turned appeasement into a pejorative term.

Conclusion

In 1919 most Britons assumed that the First World War had been the war to end wars. Few envisaged that two decades later their country would become involved in a Second World War and that when this war ended Britain would no longer be a first-class world power. So what went wrong?

Some historians regard the Second World War as simply accelerating already established trends. Arguably Britain was in retreat before 1914 and this retreat continued through the inter-war years. Given the realities of the modern world, Britain's decline was almost inevitable, whoever was in power and whatever they did. However, other historians think that the Second World War itself had a massive effect on Britain's international position. They regard Britain as a first-rate power in 1939 and think the war led to Britain's decline. Those responsible for the war are thus seen as responsible for Britain's decline.

It is certainly easy to criticise the British statesmen of the period. Lloyd George and the other main peacemakers of 1919 have frequently been condemned. The Treaty of Versailles can be seen as sowing the seeds of the Second World War. Other historians have blamed the 'appeasers' of the 1930s – Prime

Key term

Bomber deterrent Many believed that no country would risk war because of the terrible effects of aerial bombing on civilian populations.

Key dates

Treaty of Versailles: 1919

Start of Second World War: 1939

Ministers Stanley Baldwin and, especially, Neville Chamberlain. After 1945 Winston Churchill's view that Britain should have stood up to Hitler much earlier, carried, and indeed still carries, great weight.

However, many recent historians have treated the inter-war statesmen with far more sympathy and, in particular, have stressed the problems they faced. Arguably these problems were such that efforts to preserve both peace and Britain's status might have been unavailing, whoever was in power.

It should be said that few historians today would accept that events in history are inevitable. Therefore most would accept that the policies of individual statesmen did have considerable effect. But perhaps it is wrong to blame the statesmen. Perhaps most, if not all, British governments of the inter-war period acted for good and rational reasons. Perhaps Britain's position in 1945 might have been worse, but for their actions.

What is certain is that British governments after 1918, aware of Britain's vulnerability, did their best to avoid a major conflict. Their policies ultimately failed.

- Was that failure inevitable?
- Were some statesmen more responsible than others?
- Were the years 1919–39 years of retreat and decline?
- Or is it better to see the period, in historian W.N. Medlicott's words, as 'a long process of adaptation to the realities of the modern world', rather than as a period of decline?

These are questions to bear in mind as you read the rest of this book.

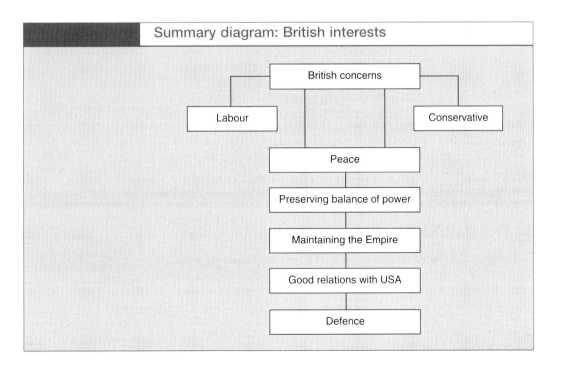

Summary diagram: British interests

2 The Versailles Peace Settlement

POINTS TO CONSIDER
This chapter should provide you with essential information about the aims of the 1919 peacemakers (especially Lloyd George), the problems they faced and the results of their work. An understanding of the peace settlement is essential if you are to make sense of Anglo-German relations in the inter-war period. You must think carefully about the criticisms of the peace settlement that were made at the time and that have been made since. Try to decide whether the peacemakers (particularly Lloyd George) should be blamed or praised for their efforts. To help your understanding, the chapter has been divided into the following themes:

• The problems of peace-making
• The aims of the peacemakers
• The main terms of the Treaty of Versailles
• The settlement of eastern Europe and Turkey

Key dates

1918	November	End of First World War
	December	British general election: victory for the Conservative–Liberal coalition. Lloyd George continued as Prime Minister
1919	January	Paris Peace Conference began
	June	Treaty of Versailles (with Germany)
	September	Treaty of St Germain (with Austria)
	November	Treaty of Neuilly (with Bulgaria)
1920	June	Treaty of Trianon (with Hungary)
	August	Treaty of Sèvres (with Turkey)
1923	July	Treaty of Lausanne (with Turkey)

1 | The Problems of Peace-making

In January 1919 the leaders of 32 countries, representing some 75 per cent of the world's population, assembled in Paris to make peace with the defeated **Central Powers**. Many criticisms have been made of the way the conference was conducted:

• the decision of the Allied leaders to participate in the work of detailed negotiation personally

Key question
What problems did the peacemakers face in 1919?

Key terms

Central Powers
Germany, Austria-
Hungary, Turkey
and Bulgaria were
known as the
Central Powers in
the First World War.

Secret diplomacy
Negotiations taking
place behind closed
doors.

Bolshevism
The Bolshevik Party
seized power in
Russia in November
1917. Led by Lenin,
the Bolsheviks
supported
communism.
Among its
opponents, the
word 'Bolshevism'
became a
derogatory term for
communism.

Big Three
Lloyd George
(Britain),
Clemenceau (France)
and Wilson (USA)
dominated the
peace-making
process. They
represented the
strongest countries
that had defeated
the Central Powers.

Key date

Paris Peace
Conference started:
January 1919

- the 'secret diplomacy'
- the fact that representatives of Russia, Germany and the other defeated powers were excluded from the peace-making process
- the fact that no agreement had been reached on the programme to be followed or how the conference was to be organised
- the domination of the small powers by the great ones.

Even the choice of Paris as a venue has been questioned: wartime passions ran higher there than in almost any other possible location. (Lloyd George had originally proposed Geneva for the venue, but had deferred in the end to French wishes – a decision he later regretted.)

Criticisms of the peace-making process have sometimes been exaggerated. However, it would be difficult to exaggerate the seriousness of the problems that the peacemakers faced.

- They somehow had to cope with a whole series of conflicting treaty commitments, promises and pronouncements which had been made during the war.
- The breakdown of the German (Hohenzollern), Russian (Romanov), Austro-Hungarian (Habsburg) and Turkish (Ottoman) empires had resulted in economic chaos, famine and outbursts of nationalism, sometimes violent, throughout central and eastern Europe and the Near East.
- There was the fear that **Bolshevism** might spread westwards from Russia and threaten the whole of Europe.
- The peacemakers were aware that they could not act in isolation; the peace settlement would need to reflect the intense popular feeling within their own countries.
- Decisions would have to be made quickly.

The **Big Three** each had large supporting teams of experts. All three were concerned with the main question: how to provide security for the future. But all held very different views about how to ensure a durable peace settlement. This, in part, reflected the popular pressure to which they were subjected.

The conclusion of a satisfactory peace treaty with Germany was the major concern of the Big Three. Once the Treaty of Versailles had been signed (in June 1919), Lloyd George and the other leading statesmen returned home. The completion of treaties with Germany's allies was left to less eminent Allied representatives. This was done in a piecemeal fashion between July 1919 and August 1920. The treaties with Austria, Hungary, Bulgaria and Turkey were to be as controversial (both at the time and since) as the Treaty of Versailles.

The Big Three at Versailles. From left to right: Georges Clemenceau, Woodrow Wilson and David Lloyd George.

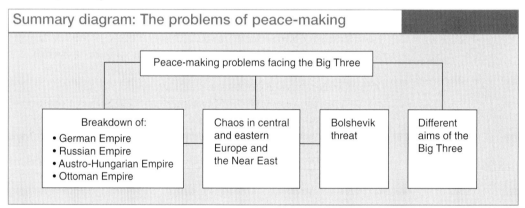

Summary diagram: The problems of peace-making

Peace-making problems facing the Big Three

Breakdown of:
• German Empire
• Russian Empire
• Austro-Hungarian Empire
• Ottoman Empire

Chaos in central and eastern Europe and the Near East

Bolshevik threat

Different aims of the Big Three

2 | The Aims of the Peacemakers

Wilson's Fourteen Points

When Germany had sought peace terms in the autumn of 1918, it had assumed these would be based on President Wilson's **Fourteen Points** that it had initially rejected when it was still hopeful of victory.

Wilson, seeking to distance himself from traditional European diplomatic dealings, had talked in terms of a peace based on justice, equality and democracy. He had later stated that the eventual peace should contain 'no annexations, no contributions, no punitive damages'. Wilson's Fourteen Points, which suggested that Germany would be treated leniently, were regarded as idealistic pipedreams by most hard-headed European statesmen. But they could not be rejected out of hand. If they were to defeat Germany, Britain and France had to retain the support of the

Key question
What were the main aims of the peacemakers (especially Lloyd George)?

Fourteen Points
President Wilson's peace programme of Fourteen Points had first been announced in a speech to the US Congress in January 1918.

USA, the world's strongest economic power. However, both Lloyd George and Clemenceau did express serious reservations about some of Wilson's ideas. They were aware that most people in Britain and France wanted revenge and a harsh peace. By November 1918 even Wilson accepted that Germany should make compensation 'for all damage done to the civilian population of the Allies'.

Clemenceau vs Wilson

Clemenceau was determined on a punitive peace. Twice in his lifetime France had been invaded by Germany. In 1871 France had lost Alsace-Lorraine and been forced to pay massive **reparations**. French casualties between 1914 and 1918, in proportional terms, were the highest sustained by the Allied powers. Clemenceau, 'The Tiger', wanted German power reduced so that all prospect of a future military threat was eliminated. In demanding security and compensation for the losses France had endured, he was asking no more than every French citizen expected.

Wilson was less interested in punishing Germany. The USA faced no immediate military threat and had no territorial or even overt economic aims. Wilson came to the peace conference still affirming general principles. He was primarily concerned with establishing a fair and lasting system of international relations. In particular, he wanted to set up a League of Nations and favoured the principle of **self-determination** for all subject peoples.

Lloyd George's aims

Lloyd George's position is more difficult to define. Although Britain had no territorial claims in Europe, Lloyd George was anxious to preserve Britain's naval supremacy and also prepared (under Conservative pressure) to enlarge the British Empire – time-honoured British objectives. Aware of the strong anti-German feeling in Britain, he had announced in the 1918 election campaign that he expected Germany to pay 'to the limit of her capacity' for the damage she had inflicted. Lloyd George was prepared to destroy **German militarism** and even support demands that **Kaiser Wilhelm II** should be hanged.

However, he distinguished between the old imperial German leaders and the German people as a whole. Germany was now ruled by parliamentary leaders. It seemed unwise to undermine their authority or to persecute them for the sins of the Kaiser. Conscious of the danger of leaving an embittered Germany, he was inclined to leniency. In the Fontainbleu memorandum of March 1919, Lloyd George wrote:

> I cannot imagine any greater cause for future war than that the German people who have proved themselves one of the most powerful and vigorous races of the world, should be surrounded by a number of small states, many of them consisting of peoples who have never previously set up a stable government for themselves, but each containing large masses of Germans clamouring for reunion with their native land.

Key terms

Reparations
Compensation paid by defeated states to the victors.

Self-determination
The right of people, usually of the same nationality, to set up their own government and rule themselves.

Key date

Lloyd George, leading a Conservative–Liberal coalition, won the general election and continued as Prime Minister: December 1918

Key terms

German militarism
The German army had been a major force in Europe since 1870. Its generals exerted great political influence, particularly true during the First World War.

Kaiser Wilhelm II
Emperor of Germany from 1888 to 1918. When it was clear that Germany had lost the war, he abdicated and fled to the Netherlands.

Lloyd George also feared that if Germany was excessively humiliated it might be driven into the arms of the Bolsheviks. While he talked 'hard' for home consumption, he was prepared to act 'soft' and do all he could to ease some of the harsher terms that Clemenceau was intent on imposing.

Lloyd George has often been seen as the main architect of the Versailles settlement. It is claimed that he was in a strong position because he often found himself able to mediate between Clemenceau and Wilson. However, this is a debatable claim. It is possible to view Lloyd George, rather than Wilson, as the opponent of most of the extreme French demands. Thus, the US president could be seen as being in the best bargaining position. The records seem to suggest that the process of bargaining among the Big Three was highly complex, with attitudes by no means fixed. Certainly the final treaty was the result of a whole series of compromises on many issues. It would be wrong, therefore, to single out Lloyd George as the main arbiter of the peace settlement.

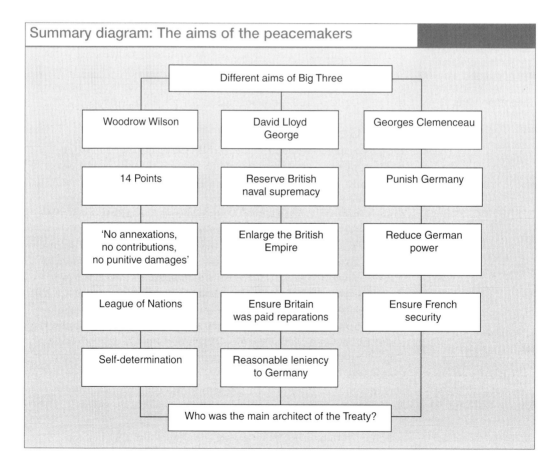

Summary diagram: The aims of the peacemakers

Different aims of Big Three

Woodrow Wilson	David Lloyd George	Georges Clemenceau
14 Points	Reserve British naval supremacy	Punish Germany
'No annexations, no contributions, no punitive damages'	Enlarge the British Empire	Reduce German power
League of Nations	Ensure Britain was paid reparations	Ensure French security
Self-determination	Reasonable leniency to Germany	

Who was the main architect of the Treaty?

Profile: David Lloyd George 1863–1945

1863 – Born in Manchester
1864 – Moved to Llanystumdwy in Wales
1884 – Passed law examinations
1890 – Elected as Liberal MP
1905 – Cabinet minister as President of the Board of Trade
1908 – Became Chancellor of the Exchequer: responsible for introducing old age pensions and National Insurance: he also took the lead in limiting the powers of the House of Lords
1915 – Became Minister for Munitions
1916 – Became Prime Minister
1918 – Widely regarded as 'the man who won the war', he also won the December election but was now dependent on Conservative support
1919 – Attended Paris Peace Conference
1922 – Chanak Crisis (see pages 31–2): resigned as Prime Minister when the Conservatives left his coalition government; never again held office
1945 – Died

Lloyd George had critics at the time, and since. J.M. Keynes, the economist, portrayed him as a political chameleon, 'rooted in nothing', 'void and without content'. He has been attacked for ignoring the views of his Cabinet colleagues and for refusing to delegate. Some historians have concluded that his principal aim at Versailles was simply to win popularity at home. Others have argued that he was devious, unscrupulous and delighted in improvisation; so much so that for him, the means justified themselves almost irrespective of the ends.

However, Lloyd George also had and has his supporters. Some regard him as the most inspired and creative British statesman of the twentieth century. Historian A.J.P. Taylor thought him, 'The greatest ruler of Britain since Oliver Cromwell'. Many historians see him as charting a tricky and skilful course at Paris in 1919 between the opposing views of Clemenceau and Wilson, while at the same time trying (with great success) to preserve British interests. His defenders claim that, of all the peacemakers, he had the most realistic and idealistic post-war vision to reinforce his spell-binding skills as a negotiator.

3 | The Main Terms of the Treaty of Versailles

The Treaty of Versailles was completed in great haste at the end of April 1919 and when it was rushed to the printers nobody had actually read the 440 clauses in full. The Germans, who were allowed only three weeks to make written observations, attacked nearly every provision. In the end, however, Germany had no option but to accept the treaty or face the threat of invasion. The Treaty of Versailles was finally signed on 28 June 1919.

Key question
Was Germany harshly treated?

Key date
The Treaty of Versailles: June 1919

Territorial changes

Negotiations about Germany's frontiers, both in the east and in the west, were highly contentious. The French at first demanded that the western frontier of Germany should be fixed on the River Rhine. The area on the left bank would go to France or become an independent **buffer state**. Lloyd George and Wilson both opposed this idea, believing it would become a cause of constant German resentment. Clemenceau pressed hard but failed to get his way. He was appeased by the promise of an Anglo-American defensive guarantee whereby both countries would provide military support for France.

It was also agreed that Germany should return Alsace-Lorraine to France, Northern Schleswig to Denmark, and Eupen and Malmedy to Belgium. Although the Rhineland was not divorced from Germany, it was to be occupied by Allied troops for 15 years and was to remain permanently **demilitarised**. The Saar region

Key terms

Buffer state
A neutral country lying between two others whose relations are, or may become, strained.

Demilitarised
Not occupied by military forces.

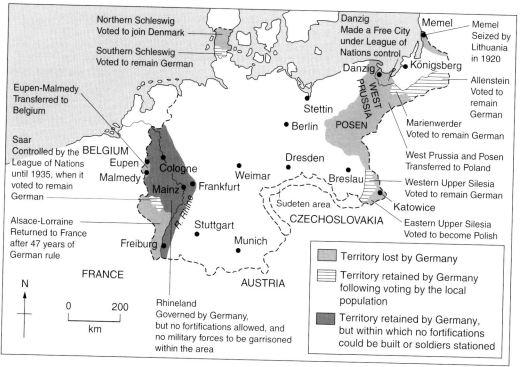

Figure 2.1: The Treaty of Versailles

Plebiscite
A vote by the people on one specific issue – like a referendum.

Polish Corridor
A small stretch of land, including the city of Danzig, which gave Poland access to the Baltic Sea but cut off East Prussia from the rest of Germany.

was placed under the control of the League of Nations for 15 years, during which time the French could work its coal mines. A **plebiscite** would then be held to decide the area's future.

The settlement of Germany's eastern border caused even more problems. The Fourteen Points had promised to create an independent Poland that would be given free and secure access to the sea. Germany could, therefore, expect to lose land to Poland. However, it was difficult to determine which land this should be because there was no clear-cut division between areas of German and Polish majority population in eastern Germany. The French wanted a strong Poland and supported the most extreme Polish territorial claims. But Lloyd George, fearful of incorporating millions of embittered Germans within the new state, fought to keep Poland as small as possible. It was because of his pressure that the key port of Danzig was made a Free City under the League of Nations and that a plebiscite was held (in 1921) in Upper Silesia, with the result that only about one-third of the area went to Poland.

The Germans were outraged by the loss of land to Poland, especially the loss of the **Polish Corridor**. Germany also lost Memel to Lithuania. Moreover, it was forbidden to unite with the Germanic 'rump' state of Austria. Had it been allowed to do so, Germany would have been greater in area and population (and thus in potential military strength) than it had been in 1914. However, this decision merely reinforced the belief that the peacemakers had made up their minds that the principle of self-determination would not be applied to Germans.

Germany's colonies

Germany lost all its colonies. Britain gained German East Africa and the Cameroons; Australia took New Guinea; South Africa acquired South-West Africa; New Zealand got Samoa; and Japan took all German possessions in China and in the Pacific north of the Equator. On Wilson's insistence, these areas were to be ruled as **mandates**. This meant that the ruling powers had to bear in mind the wishes of the colonial inhabitants who should eventually be prepared for self-government under the supervision of the League of Nations. Lloyd George was not opposed to this principle, which he described as 'virtually a codification of existing British practice'. The main opposition to the idea of mandated territory came from the Dominions and Japan, who favoured outright annexation.

Mandates
The system created in the peace settlement for the supervision of all the colonies of Germany (and Turkey) by the League of Nations.

Capital ships
Warships of the largest and most heavily armoured class, for example, battleships.

Armaments

The Allies agreed that German military power should be severely reduced. Germany was to have no heavy artillery, tanks or aeroplanes, and its army was limited to 100,000 men. Germany was to have no **capital ships** and no submarines. An Allied Control Commission was set up to police these arrangements.

PEACE AND FUTURE CANNON FODDER

The Tiger : "Curious! I seem to hear a child weeping!"

Peace and future cannon fodder. What point is the cartoonist intending to make?

War guilt

Germany was forced to sign the War Guilt clause (Article 231 of the Treaty of Versailles) accepting blame for causing the war and therefore responsibility for all losses and damage:

> Germany accepts the responsibility of Germany and her allies for all the loss to which the Allied and Associated Governments and their nationals have been subjected as a consequence of the war imposed upon them by the aggression of Germany and her allies.

Reparations

Article 231 provided a moral basis for the Allied demands for Germany to pay reparations. In reality, the War Guilt clause, which was hated by Germany, had little practical effect as Germany had already accepted in the terms of the Armistice that it would make compensation for 'all damage done to the civilian population of the Allies'. The main difficulty was deciding how much Germany could and should pay, and how this money should be divided among the Allies.

Wilson wanted a reparations settlement based on Germany's ability to pay. However, the French and British publics wanted, in the words of Sir Auckland Geddes, 'to squeeze the German lemon till the pips squeaked'. This would serve the dual purpose of helping the Allied countries meet the cost of the war and also keep Germany financially weak for years to come.

Lloyd George was pulled several ways. He was determined that Britain should get a fair share of reparations and insisted (successfully) that 'damage' should include merchant shipping losses and the costs of pensions to those disabled, widowed or orphaned by the war. Like Wilson, however, he thought that Germany should pay only what it could reasonably afford and he accepted the view that if Germany was hit too hard it would no longer be a good market for British goods, which would damage the post-war British economy. However, whatever his own feelings, Lloyd George could not afford to ignore the prevailing mood in Britain or the fact that in the 1918 election, he himself had promised to screw Germany 'to the uttermost farthing'.

Astronomical reparation figures were bandied about. In the end, at Lloyd George's suggestion, a Reparations Commission was set up to determine the amount. This effectively postponed an immediate decision and allowed tempers to cool. In 1921 the Reparations Commission finally recommended a sum of £6600 million (of which Britain was to get some 22 per cent). Although this was far less than originally envisaged, some economists and most Germans claimed (probably wrongly) that it was more than Germany could afford.

The League of Nations

The League of Nations was written into the Treaty of Versailles. This was Woodrow Wilson's obsession. He had believed (quite wrongly) that Britain and France would oppose the idea of the League. Although neither Lloyd George nor Clemenceau was an enthusiastic advocate, both were prepared to support the concept of the League in return for the friendship of the USA. Indeed the British Foreign Office, inspired by Lord Robert Cecil (Deputy Foreign Secretary) and Jan Smuts (South African Minister of Defence) had prepared a concrete scheme for the League, whereas the Americans had come to Paris 'armed' only with rather vague and woolly ideas. The British scheme became the framework for the League of Nations. The Allies had different views about the way that the League should operate but they all agreed that Germany should not be allowed to join until it had given solid proof of its intention to carry out the peace terms.

Summary diagram: The terms of the Treaty of Versailles

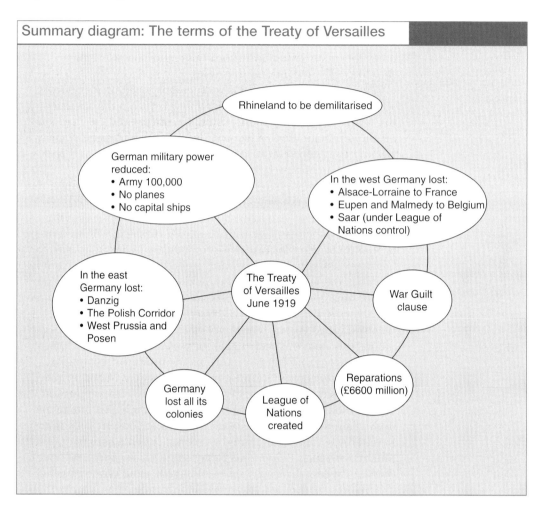

4 | Key Debate

How justified are the criticisms of Versailles?

In 1919 the Treaty of Versailles was generally well received in Britain and passed through Parliament with overwhelming majorities. On the whole Britain seemed to have gained what it had wanted from the peace settlement. German naval power had been destroyed (the German fleet scuttled itself in **Scapa Flow** in June 1919). Britain and its Dominions had acquired German colonies and Germany had agreed to pay reparations. The prevailing British view was that the treaty was firm but just.

Scapa Flow
A major British naval base in the Orkney Islands.

Key term

Criticism of the treaty

This was not the prevailing view in Germany. Germans of all political persuasions claimed that the treaty was punitive and unfair, and a major departure from Wilson's Fourteen Points, which they had been led to believe would be the basis of the peace settlement. Radical opinion in Britain soon reached the same conclusion. In 1919 the economist J.M. Keynes wrote a devastating critique of the treaty in an influential book, *The Economic Consequences of the Peace*. He argued that a naive Wilson had been forced by a vindictive Clemenceau and the scheming Lloyd George to agree to an over-harsh peace. He particularly condemned the undesirability and unworkability of the reparations clauses. Ironically, even Lloyd George had doubts about the treaty and suspected that Germany had been treated unfairly. These doubts were to be echoed by many other British politicians in the years ahead.

However, most of France considered the treaty far too soft. After a long and costly war, for which it was largely responsible, Germany had lost only 13 per cent of its pre-war territory and 10 per cent of its population. Germany had escaped division, was now surrounded only by small, unstable states on its southern and eastern borders, and remained potentially the strongest state in Europe. Clemenceau had been prepared to accept the Versailles terms only because Wilson and Lloyd George had offered France a defensive alliance. The US Senate, however, refused to sanction this alliance. The British government then did likewise. Most French people, in consequence, felt betrayed.

Historians have often echoed these contemporary criticisms. Many have claimed that the treaty was the worst of all worlds: too severe to be permanently acceptable to most Germans, and too lenient to constrain Germany for long, particularly without effective enforcement. Some historians, such as A.J.P. Taylor, have gone as far as to claim that it was the Allies' failure to solve **the German problem** in 1919 that laid the foundation of the Second World War.

Defence of the treaty

However, not all historians have been so critical and some (such as Paul Kennedy and Anthony Adamthwaite) have been prepared to defend both the peacemakers and the treaty. They have stressed the problems that Lloyd George and his fellow peacemakers faced in 1919. While they have agreed that the German problem was not solved, they have pointed out that, even with hindsight, it is difficult to suggest realistic solutions to that problem. They have claimed that the overriding problem was not so much the terms of Versailles, but rather German hostility to the treaty because it represented a defeat that most Germans were not willing to acknowledge. Even a treaty based on the Fourteen Points would not have been acceptable to Germany because it would have involved the loss of land to Poland. A really severe treaty was out of the question given Wilson's and Lloyd George's desire for a just settlement. In the circumstances Adamthwaite sees Versailles as a 'brave attempt to deal with intractable, perhaps insoluble problems'.

The Big Three, jumping from question to question and under severe domestic pressures, were not unaware of the deficiencies in their handiwork. But this was precisely why, so far as Lloyd George was concerned, the League of Nations was created. In 1919 he said that it would 'be there as a Court of Appeal to

---

Key term

The German problem
Since 1871 Germany had been the strongest nation in central Europe with the potential to control the whole of Europe. The First World War was fought in order to contain Germany. The Treaty of Versailles reduced but did not destroy Germany's potential power. The German problem was essentially Germany's power.

readjust crudities, irregularities, injustices'. This was perhaps putting too much faith in an organisation that lacked enforcement powers. Moreover (and Lloyd George did not realise this in 1919), the League was also to lack the USA. The US Senate refused to ratify the Treaty of Versailles and thus America did not become a member of the League. The result, according to historian W.N. Medlicott, was that 'Britain and France were left as the embarrassed nursemaids of a rather endearing spastic infant, the product of some injudicious international love making'.

Conclusion

Arguably the Versailles settlement fell between two stools in that it was both too harsh and too soft. While giving Germany a sense of grievance, it left it with the potential strength to redress those grievances in the future. It is thus possible to blame the Versailles peacemakers for the Second World War. But is this fair? It is clear that Lloyd George, Wilson and Clemenceau faced a host of possibly intractable problems. They did their best, in difficult circumstances, to resolve them. Is it really fair to blame them for something that happened two decades later?

Some key books in the debate

A. Adamthwaite, *The Making of the Second World War* (Routledge, 1977).

P.M.H. Bell, *The Origins of the Second World War in Europe* (Longman, 1986).

M.L. Dockrill, *Peace without Promise: Britain and the Peace Conferences 1919–23* (Batsford, 1981).

P. Kennedy, *The Realities Behind Diplomacy* (Fontana, 1981).

A. Lentin, *Guilt at Versailles: Lloyd George and the pre-History of Appeasement* (Methuen, 1985).

S. Marks, *The Illusion of Peace: International Relations in Europe, 1918–33* (Macmillan, 2003).

A. Sharp, *The Versailles Settlement: Peacemaking in Paris, 1919* (Macmillan, 1991).

5 | The Settlement of Eastern Europe and Turkey

Eastern Europe posed severe difficulties for the peacemakers. By late 1918 the **Habsburg Empire** had fallen apart. Countries such as Poland and Czechoslovakia already effectively existed. Russia, in the hands of the Bolsheviks and in the throes of a civil war, had no representatives at the peace conference, and little involving the country could be settled.

France, Britain and the USA had divergent, but not completely dissimilar, aims in eastern Europe. Some British and French statesmen would have liked to retain the Habsburg Empire in some form, if only as a potential counter-weight to Russia and Germany. But given the intense nationalist feeling among the peoples of the former empire, this was impossible. France

Key question
How successful was the settlement of eastern Europe?

Habsburg Empire
Until 1918 the Austro-Hungarian Empire, ruled for centuries by the Habsburg family, controlled large areas of central and eastern Europe.

Key term

Figure 2.2: The settlement of eastern Europe.

supported the creation of sizeable, economically viable and
strategically defensible states, which they hoped would be strong
enough to withstand either German or Russian pressure. Britain
had no wish to produce a settlement that left large numbers of
Germans outside Germany, but was concerned that the new states
should be strong enough to resist Bolshevik pressure. On the

whole, most Allied statesmen supported the US principle of self-determination and efforts were made to redraw the frontiers of eastern Europe along ethnic lines.

However, the mixture of national groups in eastern Europe meant that the establishment of frontiers was certain to cause massive problems. To make matters worse, while the peacemakers in Paris tried to redraw national boundaries, various ethnic groups in eastern Europe battled it out in a series of military confrontations. The borders that finally came into existence owed as much to the outcome of these clashes as to the negotiations at Paris.

The eastern European treaties

Ultimately, treaties were signed with Austria (the Treaty of St Germain), Hungary (the Treaty of Trianon) and Bulgaria (the Treaty of Neuilly). All the defeated powers had to pay reparations and lost large slices of territory. Austria, for example, lost land to Poland, Czechoslovakia, Italy and Yugoslavia, with the result that her population was reduced from 28 million to less than eight million.

The eastern treaties, combined with various settlements along the Russian borderlands, ultimately created a string of new states from Finland to Yugoslavia (see Figure 2.2 on page 29), whose disputes over exact frontiers continued well into the 1920s. Although the peacemakers did their best to apply the principle of self-determination, all over eastern Europe large communities found themselves governed by people of a different ethnic group. Czechoslovakia, for example, had a population of about 14,500,000, made up of Czechs, Slovaks, Germans, Hungarians, Ruthenians and Poles. Yugoslavia was even more mixed. Nothing short of massive population transfers could have resolved the problem.

Key dates

Treaty of St Germain (with Austria): September 1919

Treaty of Neuilly (with Bulgaria): November 1919

Treaty of Trianon (with Hungary): June 1920

The results

British politicians throughout the 1920s shared Lloyd George's view that the eastern frontiers were unsound and the new (or enlarged) states were unstable and unreliable. Bulgaria, Hungary and Austria were left bitter and resentful and there were social, economic and political tensions in almost every eastern European state. The fact that many of the new states contained large minorities of discontented Germans was a further problem. It seemed likely, at some time in the future, that Germany would press for territorial modifications, especially with Poland. British governments, therefore, were reluctant to commit themselves to defend the territorial settlement in eastern Europe. The best that could be hoped for was that some peaceful means could be found to revise a flawed settlement.

Key term

Ottoman Empire
Ottoman rulers controlled Turkey and a considerable amount of territory in the Middle East.

The Turkish settlement

Britain had a greater interest in the Middle East than in eastern Europe and in consequence took a greater part in deciding the fate of the **Ottoman Empire**. The Treaty of Sèvres, signed in 1920, satisfied most of Britain's concerns.

Key question
How satisfactory was the Turkish settlement?

Key term

The Straits
Comprising the
Bosphorus and the
Dardanelles, these
form the outlet
from the Black Sea
to the
Mediterranean.

Key dates

Treaty of Sèvres:
August 1920

Treaty of Lausanne:
July 1923

- **The Straits**, linking the Black Sea and the Mediterranean, were to be demilitarised and placed under international supervision.
- Large parts of the Arab areas of the Ottoman Empire were given (as mandates) to Britain and France. France acquired what is today Syria and Lebanon. Britain acquired present-day Israel, Jordan and Iraq.
- Eastern Thrace, the Gallipoli peninsula, Smyrna and several Aegean islands were given to Greece.

The Chanak crisis

In 1919–20 Mustafa Kemal, a Turkish war hero, led a national uprising. Kemal's aim was to liberate his country from continuing Allied military control and Greek occupation in the west. He rallied the various movements for Turkish liberation around his leadership and by April 1920 was able to convene a Turkish Grand National Assembly that elected him head of government.

Lloyd George, who had no love for the Turks, saw no reason to recognise Kemal's authority. In March 1921, Greece, with Lloyd George's tacit approval if not active encouragement, declared war on Kemal's government. Britain confined her aid to moral support, and the Greeks failed to make much headway. Kemal meanwhile came to terms with Italy, France and the USSR. In 1922 Turkish forces launched a major offensive in Asia Minor. Greek resistance quickly collapsed and it soon became apparent that the Turks might threaten the British forces occupying the international zone of the Straits.

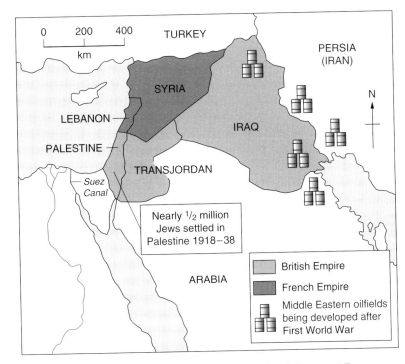

Figure 2.3: The Middle East mandates shared by Britain and France (former possessions of the Ottoman Empire).

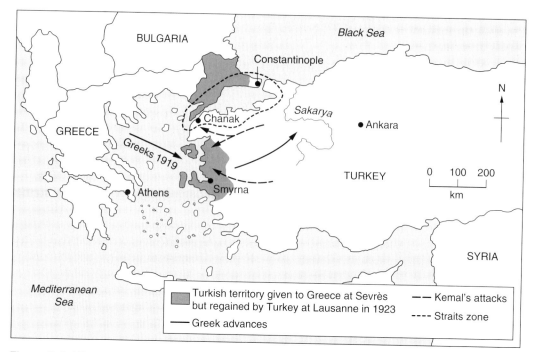

Figure 2.4: War between Greece and Turkey 1920–2.

Lloyd George seemed prepared to go to war to defend the Straits, even though Britain could expect no help from France and only lukewarm support from the British Dominions. At the end of September Turkish forces reached Chanak, the British base. Military confrontation was only avoided because of the cool judgement of the British commanders on the spot. The Turks, who had no wish to go to war with Britain, agreed to respect the international zone. Some saw the Chanak crisis as an example of successful firmness in the face of aggression and thus a victory for Lloyd George. But others saw the whole affair as unnecessary war-mongering on Lloyd George's part and the Chanak crisis contributed to his downfall in October 1922.

The Treaty of Lausanne
In the long term, the British stand at Chanak had little effect. Negotiations with Kemal's government were skilfully handled by Lord Curzon, the Foreign Secretary, and a new agreement, the Treaty of Lausanne, was signed in 1923. This was the first significant revision of the **peace settlement**.

- Turkey retained eastern Thrace, Smyrna and the Aegean islands it had won back from Greece.
- Turkey no longer had to pay reparations, but accepted the loss of its Arab territories and agreed that the Straits should remain demilitarised and open to the ships of all nations in time of peace.

Britain's main interests were thus preserved. Moreover relations with Turkey now considerably improved. Britain, therefore, had good reason to be satisfied with the new settlement.

Peace settlement
This term comprises all the different peace treaties, including the Treaty of Versailles.

Key term

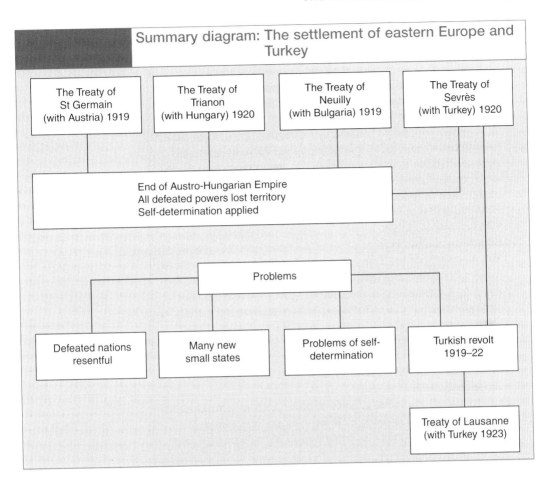

Summary diagram: The settlement of eastern Europe and Turkey

The Treaty of St Germain (with Austria) 1919

The Treaty of Trianon (with Hungary) 1920

The Treaty of Neuilly (with Bulgaria) 1919

The Treaty of Sevrès (with Turkey) 1920

End of Austro-Hungarian Empire
All defeated powers lost territory
Self-determination applied

Problems

Defeated nations resentful

Many new small states

Problems of self-determination

Turkish revolt 1919–22

Treaty of Lausanne (with Turkey 1923)

Study Guide: Advanced Level Questions

In the style of Edexcel

1. 'Lloyd George bears the main responsibility for the flawed Treaty of Versailles'. To what extent would you agree with this comment? (60 marks)

2. How far can the role of Lloyd George at the Paris Peace Conference be judged as a success? (60 marks)

> **Exam tips**
> The cross-references are intended to take you straight to the material that will help you to answer the questions.
>
> 1. There are two main issues here:
>   - To what extent was Lloyd George responsible for the Treaty of Versailles?
>   - Was the Treaty of Versailles flawed?
>   You will need to examine the peace-making process. What were Lloyd George's aims (pages 19–20)? Were his aims sensible? Why was it unlikely that he would be able to achieve all his aims? You will need to examine the different aims of the other two members of the Big Three: Woodrow Wilson and Georges Clemenceau (pages 18–19). Given the different aims of the Big

Three, some form of compromise peace was probably inevitable. To what extent did Lloyd George get his way (page 26)? Could he have done more to have achieved his aims? You will then need to consider whether the Treaty of Versailles was flawed. If so, what were its main flaws? Some historians think the Treaty was very much responsible for the outbreak of the Second World War in 1939. Is it fair to blame Lloyd George and the other 1919 peacemakers for something that happened 20 years later? It is generally wise to commit yourself in the first paragraph to the argument you are going to take in the rest of the essay. You clearly need to assess Lloyd George's role at Paris. Do you intend to blame or praise him?

2. What criteria would you employ in assessing the success (or otherwise) of Lloyd George's role at the Paris Peace Conference? You might include his aims (pages 19–20), the problems he faced (page 17), his relations with Clemenceau and Wilson (page 20), and then consideration of the extent to which he realised his aims (pages 22–6). The question might be approached in the following way:

    *   Begin with a short introductory paragraph describing the approach you intend to follow. Indicate some of the various assessments that historians have made. What is your verdict going to be?
    *   You should then write a series of paragraphs (possibly four to six), each one assessing a different aspect of the issue. Decide which issues – or criteria – you will select as paragraph points.
    *   Lloyd George's aims are clearly of crucial importance. Did he achieve most of his aims?

    You must write a concluding paragraph, of at least half a dozen sentences, which draws together the major points you have made in order to give an overall judgement. This final judgement needs to explore the extent of Lloyd George's success in the light of the problems he faced.

In the style of OCR

Study the following four passages A, B, C and D, about British attitudes to the Treaty of Versailles, and answer both the sub-questions that follow.

Passage A

From: Lloyd George's March 1919 Fontainebleau memorandum. Prime Minister Lloyd George provides information about his aims at the Paris Peace Conference.

When nations are exhausted by wars in which they put forth all their strength and which leave them tired, bleeding and broken, it is not difficult to patch up a peace that may last until the generation which experienced the horrors of war has passed away. Pictures of heroism and triumph only tempt those who know nothing of the suffering and terrors of war. It is therefore comparatively easy to patch up a peace which will last for 30 years.

What is difficult, is to draw up a peace which will not provoke a fresh struggle … You may strip Germany of her colonies, reduce her armaments to a mere police force and her navy to that of a fifth rate power; all the same in the end if she feels that she has been unjustly treated in the peace of 1919 she will find means of exacting retribution.

Passage B

From: K.O. Morgan, Consensus and Disunity: The Lloyd George Coalition Government 1918–22, *published in 1979. Morgan is a historian who believes that the appeasement of Germany followed by Lloyd George was more balanced than Neville Chamberlain's policy of appeasement.*

More than any other peacemaker, Lloyd George was profoundly disturbed by the outcome of Versailles and was anxious for its revision. He devoted his major diplomatic efforts from 1919 to an heroic effort to undo the damage it caused to European commerce and political stability. What is vital about Lloyd George's appeasement, as compared with that of Neville Chamberlain, is that he recognised that concessions should be mutual and not offered indiscriminately in response to German pressure. He recognised there was a legitimate French problem, after devastating invasions in 1870 and 1914. Some military guarantee of French territory was essential. He sought a balanced appeasement, based on strength, not surrender.

Passage C

From: Peter Clarke, Hope and Glory: Britain 1900–1990, *published in 1996. Clarke is sympathetic to Lloyd George, given the situation in 1918–19.*

All Lloyd George's instincts were for a just post-war settlement rather than vindictive retribution, especially if justice consorted with British interests … Keynes may have been right to insist that the reparations in the Versailles Treaty were uncollectable except on the unrealistic assumption of a self-denying German economic miracle; but Lloyd George secured the best deal available at the time and reckoned on the terms being revised later – as in fact happened. Other provisions of the peace treaties were similarly flawed in using the high rhetoric of liberal internationalism and self-determination … to justify compromises brokered between the cynicism of Clemenceau and the opportunism of Lloyd George. This was the fate of the League of Nations, intended as the linchpin of Wilson's new world order … Lloyd George became a convenient whipping boy for disappointments of which he was not the sole author.

Passage D

From: Robert Holland, The Pursuit of Greatness: Britain and the World Role, 1900–1970, *published in 1991. Holland believes that Germany was treated harshly at Versailles.*

The dominating aspect of the Paris Peace Conference was thus the co-operation of Lloyd George and Clemenceau in bending the pliable moralism of President Woodrow Wilson. Along the way the latter's Fourteen Points of January 1918, on which the Germans understood the Armistice to have been based, were progressively discarded … Why, then, did Lloyd George not try harder to wriggle off the hook of *revanche*, and instead ended up becoming bound to what even some of his own Cabinet colleagues referred to scathingly as a 'French document'? In fact he had little choice. The British looked to France for diplomatic support on a range of vital matters – support not likely to emanate from other quarters. Hence in the naval sphere there was at first the question of the destiny of the German Fleet; and although this matter was soon pre-empted when the latter scuttled itself on a cold night in Scapa Flow, there remained the traditionally envenomed controversy with the United States over 'maritime rights'. In addition to these considerations there were many decisions to be taken on territorial matters outside Europe in which Britain had a vital interest, not least in the Middle East, where the authorities in London were banking on French willingness to be fobbed off with the small change of a truncated Syria and its Lebanese outhouse. If France was to help Britain achieve her aims in matters such as these, the latter had no choice but to continue to assist its old partner in gaining the Continental primacy on which she appeared to be bent. This did not mean that the British premier never clashed heatedly with his French counterpart when differences arose during the Conference, but the fact remained that when Clemenceau cracked his whip, Lloyd George invariably surrendered.

1. Using these four passages and your own knowledge, assess the view that Lloyd George blundered at the Paris Peace Conference in 1919. (30 marks)
2. Assess the view that the Versailles peace settlement laid the foundation of the Second World War in Europe. (45 marks)

Exam tips

The cross-references are intended to take you straight to the material that will help you to answer the questions.

1. It is vital that you make use of all four passages. Take note on just how much the introduction to each of the passages tells you about the contents. These are the key guides as to the approach and importance of the four passages. Remember that paraphrasing the passages is a waste of time. Using reference passages does not merely mean quoting them to illustrate a point. Nor should you just deal with the issues in each one.

Good answers will arrange the issues thematically, cross-referencing the passages (for example, B and C agree whereas D does not) and using other knowledge to judge between alternative views to decide which has greater support from the evidence. With this in mind consider the following:

- What does Passage A tell us about Lloyd George's aims? Were those aims sensible? Is there any reason to doubt that these were his aims?
- Why is Passage B generally supportive of Lloyd George's role at the Peace Conference?
- Why is Passage C similarly supportive of Lloyd George's efforts? To what extent is this passage different to Source B?
- Why is Passage D critical of Lloyd George? Is Holland's criticism of Lloyd George fair? (pages 27–8)

When you have assembled your material along these lines, you can then cross-reference the passages and use your own knowledge to suggest whether or not Lloyd George did blunder at Paris. Was the Treaty of Versailles a disaster or a reasonable achievement in the circumstances? Do not leave your final evaluation to a concluding sentence or two. Try to integrate your assessment of the value of the passages into the body of your answer as you go along.

2. In many respects this question, at this stage, is unfair! Until you have read the next five chapters you will probably be unable to see the 'whole picture'. However, the question does ask you to focus on the problems created by the peace settlement. What were those problems? To what extent were the main peacemakers responsible for the problems? What could or should the peacemakers have done?

- These questions may well be part of your introduction. The first few paragraphs should then go on to consider the Treaty of Versailles (pages 22–6).
- Why did the Treaty anger most Germans (pages 26–7)?
- Was there ever any real prospect of meeting the demands of the victorious powers and satisfying German hopes? In the event was the Treaty a reasonable compromise (pages 26–8)?

Remember that there was more to the peace settlement than just the Treaty of Versailles. To what extent were other aspects of the peace settlement (not least the situation in eastern and central Europe) likely to cause future problems (pages 28–30)? You will need to reach a conclusion. Was A.J.P. Taylor right? Were the Versailles peacemakers largely responsible for the Second World War? Or is it fairer to argue that they faced a series of intractable problems? Is it really fair to blame them for something that happened two decades later?

Finally remember that evidence should be used in essay answers to evaluate the historical debate.

3 The Illusion of Peace 1919–31

POINTS TO CONSIDER

From 1919 to 1922 Lloyd George took a leading role in foreign affairs: his Foreign Secretaries very much played second fiddle. He pursued an active – indeed at times aggressive – foreign policy that almost resulted in war with Turkey in 1922. His successors' conduct of foreign policy (pre-1937) was far less dynamic. The aim of Prime Ministers Bonar Law, Baldwin and MacDonald can be summed up in one word: tranquillity. Concerned with economic and social problems at home, they rejected adventurism abroad. All hoped for a passive and cheap foreign policy. Moreover, Baldwin delegated huge responsibility to his Foreign Secretary, Austen Chamberlain. From 1919 to 1931 there was no real challenge to the status quo and thus no serious threat of war. However, British statesmen did have to deal with various problems. They did so with varying degrees of success. This chapter will examine the main problems encountered by British statesmen in the period 1919–31 through the following themes:

- Anglo-Soviet relations
- The problem of Italy
- The German question in the 1920s
- The League of Nations
- Disarmament

Key dates

1922	February	Washington Naval Agreement
	October	Lloyd George resigned; Bonar Law became Prime Minister
	October	Mussolini seized power in Italy
1923	January	French and Belgium troops occupied the Ruhr
	May	Bonar Law resigned; Baldwin became Prime Minister
	December	General election: Labour leader MacDonald became Prime Minister
1924	February	Britain recognised the Soviet government
	August	Dawes Plan

	October	General election: Conservative leader Baldwin became Prime Minister
1925		Locarno conference
1926		Germany joined the League of Nations
1929	May	General election: MacDonald became Prime Minister
	August	Young Plan

Key question
How far did a fear of Bolshevism influence British foreign policy in the period 1917–31?

Key term

Proletarian
The poorest labouring class in society.

1 | Anglo-Soviet Relations 1917–31

The Bolshevik Revolution

Britain's response to the abdication of Tsar Nicholas II in March 1917 generally had been positive. At last it seemed Russia might join the ranks of the genuine parliamentary democracies. However, the coming to power of Lenin and the Bolshevik Party in November 1917 was greeted with a more mixed reaction. Many on the British left sympathised with communism and extolled the **proletarian** triumph. But public opinion seems to have been hostile, especially when Lenin made peace with Germany at the Treaty of Brest-Litovsk in March 1918, thus enabling the Germans to concentrate all their forces on the Western Front. This anger intensified when the Bolshevik government nationalised all foreign enterprises in Russia without compensation and made it clear that they had no intention of repaying Russia's war debts due to Britain.

British hostility to Bolshevism 1918–20

Most Conservative and Liberal MPs were implacably opposed to Lenin and agreed with Minister of Munitions Winston Churchill when he spoke of 'the foul baboonery of Bolshevism'. Churchill was all for sending British forces into Russia to destroy the Bolsheviks before they could sow the seeds of revolution elsewhere in the world, possibly even in Britain. From 1918 to 1920 British government policy was one of outright hostility to the Bolshevik regime.

In March 1918 Britain sent troops to Murmansk and Archangel to ensure that war supplies that had been sent there did not fall into Bolshevik hands. As Russia plunged into civil war, British troops began to co-operate with '**White**' forces that were trying to topple Lenin and the '**Reds**'. Although Churchill and other Cabinet ministers fully supported this interventionist policy, Lloyd George was more cautious, particularly after the armistice with Germany. He tended to the view that the Russians should resolve their own internal crisis. However, anxious to retain Conservative support, he did send some military help (about 30,000 troops in all) and considerable financial assistance (some £100 million) to the Whites. For a time it seemed possible that the Whites might succeed. However, by the end of 1919 the Bolsheviks had established control in Russia (although no major power yet recognised them) and British forces were withdrawn.

Key terms

Whites
Various Russian opponents of the Bolsheviks.

Reds
Bolshevik soldiers or supporters.

The British left and Bolshevik Russia

Left-wing opinion, including the Labour Party and the **Trades Union Congress**, had condemned British intervention in Russia, representing it as a capitalist attack on the proletariat.

In 1920 Polish forces tried to take over the Ukraine from Russia. The Bolsheviks fought back and the Red Army looked as though it might capture Warsaw, the Polish capital. The British government considered sending help to Poland. The Labour movement again opposed any kind of British intervention. London dockers refused to load a ship carrying munitions already bought by the Polish government. Some 350 Councils of Action sprang up throughout Britain and even moderate Labour supporters seemed ready to support a **general strike** in a 'Hands off Soviet Russia' campaign. However, the Poles, with French assistance, succeeded in driving back the Soviet forces and Russia and Poland now made peace. British intervention, therefore, was no longer an issue and the domestic crisis ended.

The left wing in Britain had considerable sympathy for the communist 'experiment' in Russia. The British Communist Party actively identified its aims with those of the Bolsheviks. Although it was very small (it had only 4000 members in 1920), many trade unionists, rank and file Labour supporters and radical intellectuals (such as H.G. Wells and George Bernard Shaw) were ready to applaud the Russian 'workers' state', especially at a time of considerable industrial unrest at home. Some hoped for a proletarian revolution within Britain.

However, Ramsay MacDonald and other leaders of the Labour Party were highly suspicious of the anti-democratic and violent nature of Bolshevism and drew a clear distinction between **socialism** and **communism**.

Lloyd George and Russia 1920–1

By 1920–1 MacDonald held not dissimilar views to Lloyd George. The Prime Minister still had little enthusiasm for Lenin. But he now believed that wooing Russia back into a commercial relationship with Europe would have far more effect in softening the Bolshevik regime than a policy of armed intervention. In a Commons debate in 1920 he went so far as to say that the moment trade was established 'Communism would go'.

However, many of Lloyd George's Conservative supporters wished to see the USSR (as Russia was re-named in 1922) kept in diplomatic isolation and continued to remain deeply suspicious of the Bolsheviks' intentions. There was some substance to these fears. Lenin and many other communists hoped that other European countries would follow Russia's example. The **Comintern** – 'the general staff of world revolution', according to Lenin – was founded in 1919 precisely to achieve this objective. The (unsuccessful) **Spartakist rising** in Germany, the establishment of (short-lived) communist regimes in Hungary and Bavaria in 1919 and the (failed) attempts to impose a communist government in Poland in 1920 lent some credibility to Lenin's

Trades Union Congress (or TUC) The main organisation of the British trade union movement. In 1920 it represented over six million workers. Most of its leaders were strongly left wing.

General strike When workers in all industries refuse to work.

Socialism A social and economic system in which most forms of private property are abolished and the means of production and distribution of wealth are owned by the community as a whole.

Communism A social theory according to which society should be classless, private property should be abolished, and the means of production and distribution should be collectively owned and controlled. Virtually all communists would describe themselves as socialists. Socialists, however, would not necessarily describe themselves as communists.

Comintern
Communist International (also known as the Third International), founded in March 1919 in Moscow in an effort to co-ordinate the actions of the Communist Parties globally. It was totally dominated by the USSR.

Spartakist rising
An attempt by communists to seize power in Germany over the winter of 1918–19. The German communists took their name from a slave who led a revolt against the Roman Empire in the first century BC. The slave revolt failed and so did the attempted German revolution.

New Economic Policy (NEP)
In 1922 Lenin backed down from the notion of total communism. His New Economic Policy allowed some private ownership.

Lloyd George resigned and Bonar Law became Prime Minister: October 1922

hopes and British Conservatives' fears. Many Conservatives also believed that Russian agents were at work stirring up anti-British feeling in India, Afghanistan and Iran.

Changes in the USSR

After 1920 Anglo-Soviet relations very much depended on which party was in power in Britain, with Conservative governments far less willing to do business with the USSR than Labour. However, policy also shifted in response to changes in Soviet objectives. In 1921 Russia suffered appalling famine, which provoked something of a U-turn in Lenin's thinking and the adoption of the **New Economic Policy**. Soviet foreign policy began to speak with two voices. The first, that of the Comintern, still preached world revolution and claimed that Britain was the spearhead of capitalist–imperialist aggression that was aiming to destroy Communism in Russia. The second, that of the Soviet government, urged the need for normal relations with those countries – including Britain – whose economic co-operation they needed. British diplomats had difficulty adjusting to this double-speak.

Conciliatory moves

In 1921–2 Lloyd George pressed ahead with negotiations with the USSR, hoping that the re-establishment of trade relations would help the ailing British economy. He also feared that if Russia continued to be treated as an outcast she might ally with the other European pariah – Germany. Such an alliance might well threaten Europe's peace and stability.

In March 1921 an Anglo-Soviet trade agreement was finally signed. Under its terms each side agreed to refrain from hostile propaganda. The Soviet government recognised in principle its obligations to private citizens in Britain who had not yet been paid for goods supplied to Russia during the war. However, Britain (along with many other nations) was still unwilling to grant full recognition to Lenin's government.

In 1922 Lloyd George tried to widen the scope of the Anglo-Russian trade treaty and to bring Russia back into the mainstream European economic system at the World Economic Conference at Geneva. He had a series of secret discussions with the Soviet delegates, but made little progress. The chief stumbling block was Russia's refusal to pay compensation for the substantial pre-war Western investment in Russia.

Lloyd George's worst fears seemed to have been realised when, in the middle of the conference, Russia and Germany announced that they had signed the Treaty of Rapallo. This brought substantial economic and military benefits to both Germany and Russia. Germany was able to produce and test new weapons in Russia – weapons that it was banned from producing in Germany. Russia received useful German technical expertise. However, despite this pact of 'mutual friendship', both Russia and Germany (to the relief of Britain and France) continued to regard each other with considerable suspicion.

Profile: James Ramsay MacDonald 1866–1937

1866	– Born, the illegitimate son of a Scottish farmgirl
1894	– While working as a journalist, he joined the Independent Labour Party
1900–5	– Secretary of the Labour Representation Committee
1906	– Elected MP
1906–12	– Secretary of the Labour Party
1911	– Elected leader of the parliamentary Labour Party
1914	– Resigned as leader of the parliamentary Labour party because of his pacifist opposition to the First World War
1918	– Lost his seat in the House of Commons
1922	– Returned to head the Labour Party, seeking to make it a 'responsible party' of government
1924	– Led Labour's first short-lived government as well as serving as Foreign Secretary
1929–31	– Prime Minister of Labour government
1931–5	– Prime Minister of the National Government
1937	– Died

MacDonald, a hard-worker and an inspiring speaker, was Britain's first Labour Prime Minister and the first Prime Minister to have no previous ministerial experience. A moderate, he believed that socialism would only come by slow, gradual stages and for much of his political career tried to show that the Labour Party was respectable. His colleagues found him secretive and aloof.

His determination to maintain the Gold Standard amid the economic crisis of 1931 led to a split in his Cabinet over the question of reducing unemployment benefits. His decision in August 1931 not to resign with his colleagues but to accept the leadership of the National Government, with Conservative and Liberal support, led to his being branded a traitor by many in the Labour Party (from which he was expelled).

After 1931 his health deteriorated and in his final period as Prime Minister, up to 1935, he was in some ways a figure of fun. (He was known in the House of Commons as 'Ramshackle Mac'.)

MacDonald tended to accept the conventional parameters of politics and economics. Nevertheless his aims in foreign policy were different from those of his Conservative opponents. He was very much opposed to war, supported disarmament and tried to develop collective security through the League of Nations. Like many others, he did not see Nazi Germany as a particular threat to Britain (see page 73).

After the fall of Lloyd George in October 1922, Foreign Secretary Lord Curzon played a more prominent role in foreign affairs. He was much less committed to economic co-operation with Russia and threatened to end the trade agreement because of the repeated Soviet violation of the undertaking to refrain from hostile propaganda. The Russian reply was conciliatory and the agreement survived. But Curzon would take no further steps towards recognising the legitimacy of the Bolshevik regime.

Ramsay MacDonald and the USSR

In 1924 the Labour Party came to power. Ramsay MacDonald, who was both Prime Minister and Foreign Secretary, immediately resumed full diplomatic relations with the USSR and was soon negotiating for a new trade treaty which he hoped would provide an increased market for Britain. The main obstacle was still the question of debts to British creditors. In August an Anglo-Soviet Agreement, on both general and commercial matters, was finally reached. There were promises of friendship and the cessation of propaganda. In the event of a satisfactory arrangement over the settlement of British debts, the British government agreed to guarantee a loan of £30 million. The agreement, said one contemporary, was merely an agreement to agree if and when the parties could agree to agree. However, many Conservatives and Liberals, suspicious of the Labour Party's **policy of rapprochement** with the USSR, saw the agreement as more important and more threatening. The Liberals withdrew their support from the minority Labour government and in the general election which followed, Labour was charged with being susceptible to communist pressure.

The Zinoviev letter

On 25 October 1924, just a few days before the general election, the *Daily Mail* published a letter, purporting to be from Gregory Zinoviev, head of the Comintern. This letter urged the British Communist Party to work for the proposed Anglo-Soviet Agreement because of the opportunities for subversion that it would provide. It also issued instructions for all types of **seditious activities**. The Conservatives used the letter as a final '**red scare**', denouncing Labour as accomplices or dupes of the communists. The forged Zinoviev letter probably made no substantial difference to the election result. Even before the letter was published, the Conservatives had succeeded in tarring the Labour Party as pandering to communism. Due largely to the collapse of the Liberal vote, the Conservatives won a resounding victory.

Anglo-Soviet problems 1924–31

Not surprisingly, Anglo-Soviet relations now deteriorated. Prime Minister Baldwin did not ratify the Anglo-Soviet Agreement. A large USSR donation to the Miners' Federation during the **General strike of 1926** led to angry protests by the British Cabinet.

Key dates

Labour leader MacDonald became Prime Minister in general election: December 1923

Britain recognised the Soviet government: February 1924

General election and Conservative leader Baldwin became Prime Minister: October 1924

Key terms

Policy of rapprochement
To renew or improve relations with someone.

Seditious activities
Actions against the state which are intended to cause disorder and trouble.

Red scare
Words and actions from politicians and the media that suggest that there is a serious communist threat.

ON THE LOAN TRAIL.

A *Punch* cartoon (29 October 1929) endorsed the Zinoviev letter. What point was the cartoonist trying to make?

The Arcos affair caused a further rift. Arcos – the All Russian Co-operative Society – was the main organisation through which Anglo-Soviet trade was conducted. A raid on its London premises in 1927 led to Baldwin accusing the USSR of using Arcos as a means of directing 'military espionage and subversive activities throughout the British Empire and North and South America'. Britain broke off diplomatic relations and ended all trade agreements.

The Labour government that came to power in 1929 restored diplomatic contacts and signed a new commercial treaty with Russia in 1930. However, it proved impossible to reach agreement over Russian debts and the possibility of British loans. No intimacy developed between the two countries. Stalin, who was

Key term

General strike of 1926

In May 1926 large numbers of British workers, from a variety of industries, went on strike. This was to support coal miners and was aided by the TUC. In the face of resolute government action, the TUC called it off after nine days.

Key date
General election and MacDonald became Prime Minister: May 1929

now effectively in control in Russia, was primarily concerned with economic development. MacDonald's government was content to see the USSR remain on the periphery of Europe.

Summary diagram: Anglo-Soviet relations 1917–31	
1917	Bolshevik Revolution
1918	Bolsheviks quit First World War, nationalise foreign enterprises and refuse to pay war debts
1918–9	Britain sends troops to support the Whites
1920–1	Russo-Polish War: British government against British trade unions
1921	Anglo-Soviet trade agreement
1922	Creation of USSR
1924	British Labour government resumed full diplomatic relations with USSR
1924	Zinoviev letter
1924	Conservatives won general election. Anglo-Soviet relations deteriorated
1927	Arcos affair: Britain broke off diplomatic relations
1929	Labour government restored diplomatic contacts

2 | The Problem of Italy

Key question
How great a threat was Mussolini in the 1920s?

Italy had looked to the peace settlement to give it the considerable amounts of territory that had been promised in 1915 when it had entered the war. This would compensate for the heavy losses in the war and help make it the great power it had so long yearned to be. However, the peace settlement failed to provide all the promised territory, and caused considerable resentment in Italy. In 1922 Benito Mussolini, leader of the Italian **Fascist Party**, seized power in Rome. He demanded revision of the peace settlement and talked of making Italy a great imperial power. He soon showed that he was prepared to involve himself in dramatic foreign policy escapades. His ambitions in the Mediterranean, which he regarded as an Italian lake, seemed to pose a direct threat to the British Empire. The Mediterranean, which provided access to the Suez Canal, was regarded by most British statesmen as a vital link in Britain's world-wide communication chain.

Key date
Mussolini seized power in Italy: October 1922

Key term
Fascist Party
An Italian nationalist, authoritarian, anti-communist movement developed by Mussolini in Italy after 1919. The word fascism is often applied to authoritarian and National Socialist movements in Europe and elsewhere.

However, for most of the 1920s the Italian leader kept a relatively low profile, only involving himself in adventures where some glory could be won on the cheap. He won some modest gains in Africa, succeeded in annexing the port of Fiume on the border with Yugoslavia, and strengthened Italy's hold over Albania. Neither Mussolini nor fascism, which appeared to be a uniquely Italian phenomenon, posed the serious threat in the 1920s that some had feared they would. Indeed, some British statesmen, including Churchill and Lloyd George, expressed admiration for Mussolini's achievements in Italy.

Profile: Benito Mussolini (1883–1945)

1883	– Born in Italy, the son of a socialist blacksmith and a school teacher
1900	– Became a radical member of the Italian Socialist Party
1912	– Became chief editor of the Socialist Party's newspaper *Avanti!* whose circulation he increased from 20,000 to 100,000 by 1914
1915	– Broke with the Socialist Party over the First World War. He passionately supported Italy's entry and founded his own newspaper *Il Popolo d'Italia* (The People of Italy)
1915–17	– Served in the war until he was wounded
1919	– Founded the *Fasci di Combattimento* (or Combat Groups) in Milan. These soon became known as the Fascist movement. Its supporters wore black shirts. Mussolini was now strongly nationalistic and bitterly anti-socialist. However, he did support social reform
1922	– Came to power following the March on Rome
1924	– Became effectively dictator in Italy: he was known as *Il Duce* (the Leader)
1929	– Signed the Lateran Agreement with the Pope, ending years of conflict between the Church and the Italian state
1935–6	– Italy at war with Abyssinia (see pages 81–2)
1936	– Rome–Berlin Axis proclaimed (see page 89)
1936–9	– Italian troops fought on Franco's side in the Spanish Civil War (page 88)
1940	– Mussolini entered the Second World War on Germany's side
1943	– Mussolini was deposed by the Fascist Grand Council and imprisoned
1943–5	– Liberated by German paratroopers, he was placed at the head of the Italian Social Republic in northern Italy
1945	– Shot by Italian partisans as he tried to flee to Switzerland

Mussolini has generally had a bad press. He was the founder of fascism and ended up supporting Hitler in the Second World War. He was not viewed so negatively for much of the 1920s and 1930s. A number of British statesmen, including Winston Churchill, spoke and wrote approvingly of his actions. He was certainly popular in Italy, where he enjoyed substantial support until 1940. He seemed to provide strong leadership and his foreign adventures gave Italians a pride in their country.

He had some economic success: Italy's GNP grew by an average of over one per cent a year between 1922 and 1940 – not a bad record in view of the Great Depression (see page 66). Many

Italians overlooked the fascist attack on political freedoms and individual liberties.

However, Mussolini's success was limited. He was, in historian Denis Mack Smith's view, a 'stupendous poseur', more concerned with projecting himself as a superman than with administrative routine. This was apt because his movement lacked the efficiency to dominate Italian society. Many Italians viewed fascism with some scepticism. There was outward conformity but little inner conviction. Fascism's impact on the economy was also limited. Italy lacked the economic strength to compete with Germany or Britain. The Second World War, which brought him down, was final proof of Mussolini's failure.

Summary diagram: The problem of Italy

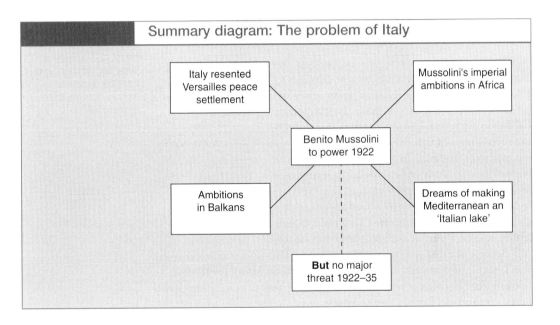

3 | The German Question in the 1920s

Allied disagreement

British foreign policy in the 1920s was dominated by the German question. In 1919 it had been generally assumed that Germany would honour the Treaty of Versailles as other defeated nations had honoured peace treaties in the past. But most Germans were determined to avoid carrying out the terms of the peace settlement. In consequence, the enforcement of the Treaty of Versailles required the same determination and co-operation among the victorious powers as winning the war had done. The reverse occurred. By the start of the 1920s Britain and France disagreed on just about everything, while the USA divorced itself from events in Europe.

French leaders were particularly concerned about Germany's efforts to undo the treaty. France had a land border with an embittered Germany – a country with 50 per cent more people and four times France's heavy industry. In this situation the French response was to insist on the most stringent enforcement of the peace terms. French governments also searched for alternative means of security.

- They did all they could to seek a firm military alliance with Britain.
- They concluded military agreements with states of eastern Europe, such as Poland (1921) and Czechoslovakia (1924). In the event of a Franco-German war, Germany would thus be surrounded.

British governments opposed most aspects of French policy. Few British statesmen actually trusted France. In 1920 a Channel Tunnel project was rejected by the Foreign Office on the grounds that 'our relations with France never have been and are not, and probably never will be, sufficiently stable and friendly to justify the building of a Channel Tunnel'. In general, British governments regarded France's efforts to encircle Germany with disapproval. Indeed, in the 1920s British Foreign Office officials feared French domination of Europe as much as they feared the possibility of a German revival of strength.

Moreover, many British politicians soon expressed misgivings about the Treaty of Versailles and the treatment of Germany. There was increasing unease about the one-sided application of self-determination (see page 23), about Germany's exclusion from the League of Nations, and about reparations. Many influential people thought that a revision of the treaty was urgently needed if there was to be a lasting peace in Europe.

Key question
Why did Britain and France disagree about how to treat Germany?

The reparations problem

In the early 1920s international relations were dominated by two topics: reparations and security. No fewer than 23 summit conferences were held between 1920 and 1922. Most followed a similar pattern. British representatives urged the French to relax the provisions of Versailles, but to little effect. French leaders feared that any treaty revision would strengthen Germany and lead to its economic and military dominance in Europe. Thus, the First World War would have been in vain and there would be the spectre of a German war of revenge.

In 1920 and 1921 French troops occupied several German cities when Germany violated the reparation and disarmament clauses of Versailles (see pages 23–5). Britain opposed such action. First Lloyd George, then Bonar Law and Baldwin, wanted to adopt policies that would appease Germany. They particularly wished to reduce German reparations payments and to promote

Bonar Law resigned and Baldwin became Prime Minister: May 1923

Key date

Germany's economic recovery in the belief that this would help British trade. France might have been prepared to take a more conciliatory line had Britain been ready to sign a military alliance with her. Most British politicians opposed this idea.

In 1922 Britain tried to resolve the reparations issue by proposing a cancellation of both reparations and the payments of war debts to the USA. This idea received little favour in America, France or even in the City in London. (Britain was owed four times as much as it owed the USA and would therefore have been a net loser if the scheme had been adopted.) Reparations, therefore, continued to sour Anglo-French and Franco-German relations.

The occupation of the Ruhr

By December 1922 Germany had fallen hopelessly behind in its reparation payments. Raymond Poincaré, the new anti-German French leader, decided that enough was enough. In January 1923 French and Belgian troops occupied the Ruhr, the industrial heart of Germany, with the intention of forcing Germany to meet its financial obligations. The occupation of the Ruhr stirred up intense feelings of German nationalist hostility against France. German authorities adopted a policy of **passive resistance**, with the result that industrial production in the Ruhr ground to a halt, the German economy collapsed and Germany suffered **hyper-inflation**.

The British government disliked, but did not openly condemn, French policy. It adopted what one contemporary described as a policy of 'surly neutrality', trying without success to resolve the crisis. Some British officials thought the Ruhr occupation was an economic disaster for Britain. In fact just the opposite was the case. British exports soared and unemployment fell as German competition disappeared. Although Poincaré faced strong British and US financial pressure, he held out stubbornly for several months, opposing any reform of the reparations settlement, supporting a **Rhineland separatist movement** (which soon collapsed), and finally forcing the Germans to abandon their policy of passive resistance in the Ruhr and to pay reparations.

The Dawes Plan

In April 1924 a reparations committee (known as the Dawes Committee after its US chairman) proposed that payments should be reduced and phased over a longer period, thus cutting the annual and total amounts to be paid in reparations. In the meantime, Germany should receive a US loan to help it over immediate difficulties.

Ramsay MacDonald, the new British Prime Minister, worked hard to secure French and German acceptance of the Dawes Plan. The replacement of Poincaré by Edouard Herriot in May 1924 helped MacDonald's cause and agreement was finally reached in August 1924. Germany agreed to meet the new reparation payments. In return, France agreed to withdraw its forces from the Ruhr within one year.

Key dates

French and Belgian troops occupied the Ruhr: January 1923

Dawes Plan: August 1924

Key terms

Passive resistance
Deliberate refusal to co-operate with the authorities. Those who support such action adopt peaceful, not violent, protest.

Hyper-inflation
A huge increase in the amount of (almost worthless) money in circulation, resulting in a massive increase in prices. In Germany in 1923 an egg cost hundreds of millions of marks.

Rhineland separatist movement
The French government hoped that German people living west of the River Rhine might split from Germany and form an independent state.

GERMANY:
"ACH! AINDT IT TOO FAR ?"

PARKER GILBERT:
"THE FIRST SEVEN MILLION
MILES ARE THE HARDEST.
AFTER THAT YOU GET USED
TO IT." (gives a hollow chuckle)

IN REPARATIONS DREAMLAND.

'In Reparations Dreamland' (a David Low cartoon). Why in the cartoon are loans shown as balloons and the financial experts shown as sinister figures? Why should a British cartoonist be sympathetic to Germany? (David Low, *Evening Standard*, 7 January 1929, Centre for the Study of Cartoons and Caricature, University of Kent.)

Both countries kept their side of the bargain. For the next few years Germany met its reparations almost in full, thanks largely to extensive US loans. Thus began a bizarre triangular flow of money between the USA and Europe. US loans enabled Germany to pay reparations to France and Britain, which in turn helped Britain and France to repay their US war debts.

Most historians consider the occupation of the Ruhr as a defeat for France. Ultimately it had been forced to accept a substantial revision of reparations and had gained nothing in return.

The Locarno Pact

The Ruhr occupation convinced many French statesmen that in future they should not attempt to enforce the Treaty of Versailles single-handed. Worried by the growing strength of Germany, they looked increasingly to Britain for guarantees of security. However, both Labour and Conservative governments were opposed to binding Britain to France and were opposed to French efforts to strengthen the coercive powers of the League of Nations. Balfour thought France's obsession with security was 'intolerably foolish … They are so dreadfully afraid of being swallowed up by the tiger that they spend all their time poking it.' Even the pro-French Austen Chamberlain, who became Foreign Secretary in

Key question
How important was
the Locarno Pact?

Key date

Locarno conference:
1925

November 1924, failed to persuade his Conservative Cabinet colleagues to accept anything in the way of an Anglo-French alliance.

However, in 1925 Chamberlain took up an offer from Gustav Stresemann, the German Foreign Minister. Stresemann said he was prepared to enter into an agreement with France for a joint guarantee of their frontiers in western Europe. Thanks largely to Chamberlain's efforts, representatives from Britain, France, Germany, Italy, Poland, Czechoslovakia and Belgium met at Locarno in Switzerland in September 1925. The terms of office of the three main participants – Chamberlain, Stresemann and Aristide Briand, the French Foreign Minister – largely coincided, and collectively they dominated European diplomacy for the remainder of the 1920s. They were all anxious to see an improvement in Franco-German relations. Therefore the Locarno meeting was a far cry from the grim tension of earlier international conferences.

The Locarno Pact consisted of a number of agreements. It was decided that Germany should be welcomed into the League of Nations in 1926. Germany's western frontiers with France and Belgium were accepted as final and were guaranteed by Britain and Italy. Stresemann, despite British and French pressure, would not agree to accept Germany's eastern boundaries. The most he would do was state that the frontiers should not be altered by force, but he even refused to put his signature to this promise. However, he was prepared to recognise the new treaties of mutual military assistance signed between France, Poland and Czechoslovakia.

The results of Locarno

At the time, the Locarno Pact was seen as a diplomatic triumph and a great landmark. Austen Chamberlain regarded it as 'the real dividing line between the years of war and the years of peace'. It seemed that Germany had been readmitted to the community of nations and that France and Germany had been reconciled. People talked of a new spirit, the 'spirit of Locarno', and Chamberlain, Briand and Stresemann were awarded the Nobel Peace Prize for their efforts.

However, many historians now tend to view Locarno in a less positive light. They point out that Germany did not abandon any of its ambitions in the east and that perhaps Britain encouraged these ambitions by indicating its unwillingness to guarantee Germany's eastern frontier. Chamberlain wrote: 'No British government ever will, or ever can, risk the bones of a British grenadier … for the Polish Corridor'.

Britain's guarantee of the western borders is also seen as little more than an empty gesture. In 1926 the British Chiefs of Staff revealed that they had no plans and few forces to give substance to the new obligations. From France's point of view Locarno was a potentially worrying agreement. It clearly represented the furthest extent Britain was prepared to go in terms of supporting the Versailles settlement – and by simply giving a general pledge against aggression in the west, Britain had not gone far. Indeed the British pledge was as much a guarantee to Germany as to France: a new French move into the Ruhr was now impossible without France breaking the Locarno Pact. In reality the Pact did not really denote any fundamental change in British policy. The British government had no intention of being drawn into Anglo-French military talks. Britain had given a guarantee that Chamberlain was convinced would never have to be honoured.

Moreover, Locarno did not end Germany's sense of grievance or its attempts to secure revision of the Treaty of Versailles. France retained its distrust of German intentions, so much so that in 1927 it began the construction of the **Maginot Line**. Regular meetings between Stresemann, Briand and Chamberlain after 1926 yielded little in the way of agreement. Chamberlain, in private, grumbled over Germany's ingratitude and its demands for further revision. Stresemann grumbled that further concessions to Germany took longer than he had anticipated.

Maginot Line French defensive fortifications stretching along the German frontier.

Key term

Improved relations

However, the Locarno Pact did improve the international atmosphere of the late 1920s. Although Stresemann was a German nationalist and determined to dismantle the Versailles settlement, he saw the advantage of collaboration with the Western powers and was prepared to work with Chamberlain and Briand through the League of Nations. In the late 1920s there seemed no real prospect of major conflict. In 1928 all the major powers signed the Kellogg–Briand Pact, renouncing war as a means of settling international disputes. (Frank Kellogg was the US Secretary of State.) The British government was happy to sign, although some Conservative British politicians thought the Kellogg–Briand Pact idealistic nonsense.

In 1929 the Young Plan extended the period of reparations payments by 60 years, thus further easing the burden on Germany. As part of this package, Britain and France agreed to end their occupation of the Rhineland five years ahead of schedule. In 1929 it seemed, as historian William Rubinstein has written, 'literally inconceivable that a second worldwide general war, far deadlier than the last, could break out only 10 years later'.

Young Plan: August 1929

Key date

Summary diagram: The German question in the 1920s

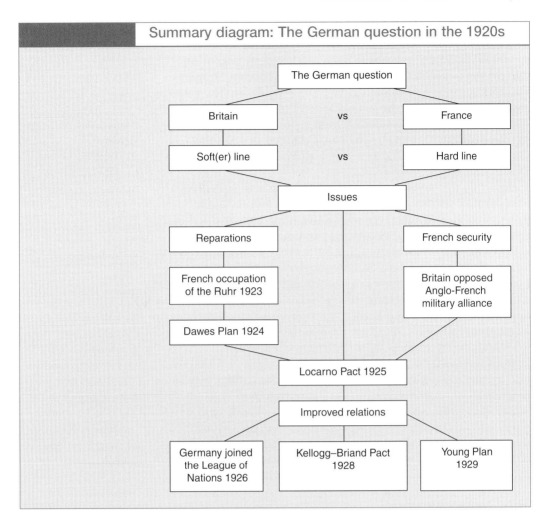

4 | The League of Nations

Key question
How effective was the League of Nations in the 1920s?

One result of the Treaty of Versailles was the creation of the League of Nations. This had its headquarters in Geneva. The Assembly of the League, composed of representatives of all the member states, met yearly and each state had one vote. Britain, France, Italy and Japan had permanent seats on the Council of the League. The Assembly could then elect four (later six) further members of the Council. The Council made most of the League's decisions. By the Covenant of the League, member states agreed to a number of (somewhat vague) articles. Perhaps the most important was Article 16, which stated that if any member of the League resorted to war, the other states should impose **economic sanctions** and, if necessary, take appropriate military action.

Key term

Economic sanctions
Refusing to trade with a particular country.

Britain and the League

Although the League of Nations owed its inception largely to Woodrow Wilson, it soon evoked enthusiastic support in Britain, especially from the left. British public opinion came to accept that the League was an institution with a ready-made machinery for solving all international problems peacefully. Many believed that no aggressor would dare to risk war with the 50 or so League states and that in consequence force would not be needed to uphold the principles of the League. British Foreign Ministers faithfully attended the meetings of the Assembly and the Council, aware that support for the League often brought popularity at home. The **League of Nations Union** soon proved to be an effective pressure group. Its chairman claimed in 1928 that 'All parties are pledged to the League … all Prime Ministers and ex-Prime Ministers support it …'.

But while they might support the League in principle, few Conservative politicians really believed in its efficacy as an instrument for solving international disputes. They realised that the League's mere existence did not automatically prevent aggression, and that without the USA and the USSR it was hardly a truly global organisation. Military leaders pointed out that the League had no armed forces of its own and warned that it created a misleading and dangerous sense of security. In reality it depended on Britain and France resisting those countries bent on aggression. But given the League's popularity, few politicians were prepared to express these criticisms openly.

From the start, the French had hoped to fashion the League into a force to preserve the Versailles boundaries. They continued to try to strengthen the League's obligations and to make them more binding on member states. On the other hand, most British politicians favoured a looser, less binding arrangement and thought the League should function as an instrument for the peaceful adjustment of international boundaries and other disputed matters, not as a force committed to oppose all change.

The Geneva Protocol

In 1923 the Assembly of the League accepted a draft treaty of Mutual Assistance designed to outlaw 'aggressive war'. This proposal was strongly opposed by both the **British Admiralty** and the **British Dominion governments**. In April 1924 the Labour Prime Minister Ramsay MacDonald, who earlier had proclaimed the determination of his party to strengthen the League, decided not to support the draft treaty. Instead, in conjunction with the French Premier, Herriot, he suggested a new scheme, the Geneva Protocol. Any state refusing to submit a dispute to **arbitration** or rejecting the decision of an arbitrator would be regarded as an aggressor and liable to be subjected to economic sanctions or even military force. There was strong British opposition to the Protocol's vague but potentially unlimited commitments and it was rejected by a new Conservative government in 1925.

The impact of the League

The League did have some successes in the 1920s. In general it established itself as an international organisation capable of resolving disputes between minor powers and promoting a wide range of humanitarian and economic activities. It was a useful talking shop and its meetings provided good opportunities for

Key terms

League of Nations Union
A British organisation set up to support the League.

British Admiralty
The government board that administered the Royal Navy.

British Dominion governments
Countries within the British Empire that were more or less self-governing. By 1922 Canada, Australia, New Zealand, South Africa and the Irish Free State all had their own parliaments. They also had seats in the Assembly of the League.

Arbitration
A way of reaching a settlement. This is usually done by submitting a case to a neutral judge or committee to decide the outcome of a dispute.

Key date

Germany joined the League of Nations: 1926

foreign statesmen to meet and discuss outside the formal sessions. The League's status seemed to be further enhanced when Germany joined in 1926.

However, the League had little real influence. The important questions of the day were settled in the hotel rooms of the Foreign Ministers of Britain, France, Italy and (after 1926) Germany, and the small states were helpless in the face of the reality of great power politics.

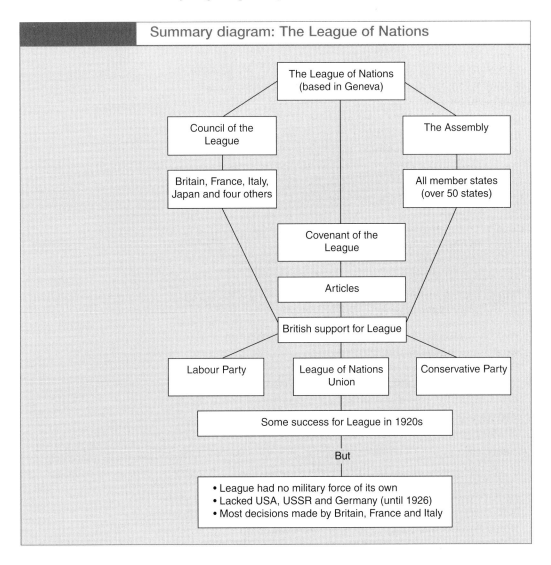

Summary diagram: The League of Nations

The League of Nations (based in Geneva)

Council of the League — Britain, France, Italy, Japan and four others

The Assembly — All member states (over 50 states)

Covenant of the League

Articles

British support for League

Labour Party — League of Nations Union — Conservative Party

Some success for League in 1920s

But

- League had no military force of its own
- Lacked USA, USSR and Germany (until 1926)
- Most decisions made by Britain, France and Italy

Key question
How successful were efforts to achieve disarmament in the 1920s?

5 | Disarmament

In 1919 the Allies had disarmed Germany, a move seen by some as the first step in the process of general world disarmament. Members of the League of Nations agreed to disarm to 'the lowest point consistent with national safety'. Most British governments in the 1920s favoured disarmament for political and economic reasons. Defence spending was cut back. By 1932

Britain was spending only £102 million on defence, compared with £760 million in 1919–20. The army reverted to its pre-war role of imperial police force and, although the RAF preserved its separate identity, it remained small in numbers. But the most interesting developments surrounded the Senior Service – the Royal Navy.

Washington Naval Agreement: February 1922

Key date

Naval disarmament

Although the war had brought about the destruction of the German fleet, in 1919 there seemed every prospect of there being a naval race between the USA and Britain. The Admiralty was furious that the US naval building programme aimed to create a fleet larger than the Royal Navy. There was also the problem of a growing Japanese fleet in the Pacific. The USA was more suspicious of Japan's intentions than Britain and was anxious to end the Anglo-Japanese treaty of 1902.

In November 1921 representatives of the main naval powers – the USA, Britain, France, Italy and Japan – met in Washington. This conference led to the conclusion of the 1922 Washington Naval Agreement under which capital ships allowed to the countries concerned would be in the following ratios: USA 5; Britain 5; Japan 3; Italy 1.75; and France 1.75. No new capital ships were to be constructed for 10 years. Britain also agreed not to renew its alliance with Japan. It was replaced by a Four Power Treaty signed by Britain, the USA, France and Japan, guaranteeing the status quo in the Far East.

There was considerable British opposition to the Washington agreement for a number of reasons:

- Britain no longer had naval superiority. The size of its fleet would now be determined by the treaty, not by an assessment of Britain's strategic needs.
- The halt in capital ship building would leave Britain with an obsolescent fleet by the time construction was allowed again.
- British interests in the Far East would no longer be protected by the Japanese alliance.

While some historians still argue that the Washington agreement was a major catastrophe for Britain, there were some advantages:

- In particular it avoided a wasteful and unnecessary naval race with the USA, the cost of which would have been enormous and which the USA almost certainly would have won.
- Although Britain had sacrificed its old relationship with Japan and had thus weakened its position in the Far East, it had at least remained on good terms with the USA – and at the end of the day this was more important than remaining on good terms with Japan.

For many politicians at the time, and historians since, the Washington naval disarmament system seemed to be a constructive and forward-looking act.

The Washington agreement was not totally successful. Throughout the 1920s there was a naval race of sorts as Britain, the USA and Japan all set about constructing non-capital ships, especially cruisers. In 1927 an attempt to limit the number of cruisers broke down. Eventually, in 1930 the USA, Britain and Japan agreed to limit their cruisers in a fixed ratio (10:10:7) and to prolong the agreement on the building of capital ships for a further five years.

Military disarmament

Securing agreement about land armaments proved far more difficult. The main problem was the relationship between France and Germany. French leaders, aware that Germany was not even complying with the disarmament terms of the Treaty of Versailles, realised that it would be national and political suicide to reduce its own large forces without watertight guarantees of security. Germany, on the other hand, demanded to be treated as an equal. A Preparatory Commission on Disarmament, set up in 1926, failed to make headway because of mutual suspicion. German demands for equality were incompatible with French demands for security. Thus, the German army continued to be limited to 100,000 men.

Britain continued to cut back its spending on its army. After 1918 the **General Staff** hoped to maintain a small, professional and well-equipped, mechanised and motorised army. The army was small and professional but unfortunately it was not particularly well equipped, mechanised or motorised. There seemed little point in spending huge sums of money on the army. There was no serious threat to Britain. The Kellogg–Briand Pact seemed to auger well for disarmament and the maintenance of world peace.

Key term

General Staff
The body that administers the British army.

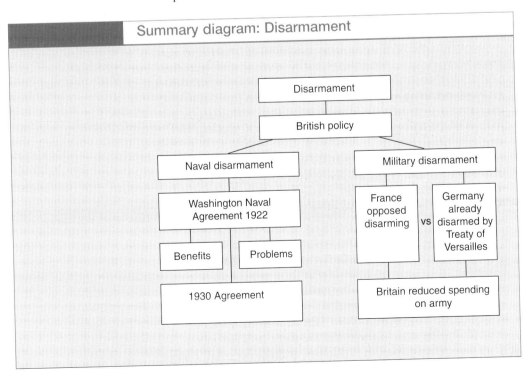

Summary diagram: Disarmament

6 | Key Debate

Was British foreign policy-making in the 1920s a success or failure?

Historians, echoing contemporary opinion, have had conflicting views about British foreign policy-making in the 1920s.

A success

It is easy to be positive about developments. At the start of the 1930s there seemed good reason for optimism. Although many outstanding questions still menaced Franco-German relations, both countries seemed ready to settle disputes by negotiation rather than by force. Mussolini's oratory was occasionally warlike, but his escapades were minor. Bolshevik Russia had turned out to be more an embarrassment than a serious problem. No great power in the 1920s had threatened the security of Britain or its Empire. In consequence, Britain, like many countries, had been able to run down its armed forces. Almost all the major powers had agreed to renounce war and the League of Nations seemed an effective organisation that would ensure peace.

In 1929 Viscount D'Abernon, British Ambassador to Germany in the mid-1920s, wrote that the lesson of the post-war years was not:

> … negative … but positive. It is not a recital of unfortunate events which led up to a great catastrophe. It is the narrative rather of a historical period in which immense progress has been made towards pacification, and during which the international suspicion diminished, and the cause of co-operation between nations appreciably advanced.

Winston Churchill, writing in 1948, summed up the 1920s in generally favourable terms.

> Although old antagonisms were but sleeping, and the drumbeat of new levies was already heard, we were justified in hoping that the ground thus solidly gained would open the road to a further forward march.
>
> At the end of the second Baldwin Administration [1929] the state of Europe was tranquil, as it had not been for 20 years, and was not to be for at least another 20. A friendly feeling existed towards Germany following upon our Treaty of Locarno, and the evacuation of the Rhineland by the French Army and Allied contingents at a much earlier date than had been prescribed at Versailles. The new Germany took her place in the truncated League of Nations. Under the genial influence of American and British loans Germany was reviving rapidly … France and her system of alliances also seemed secure in Europe. The disarmament clauses of the Treaty of Versailles were not openly violated. The German Navy was non-existent. The German Air Force was prohibited and still unborn. There were many influences in Germany strongly opposed, if only

on the grounds of prudence, to the idea of war, and the German High Command could not believe that the Allies would allow them to rearm.

A failure

However, Sally Marks, a historian, writing in 1976, had a different view.

> A few men knew that the spirit of Locarno was a fragile foundation on which to build a lasting peace. After all, the real spirit at Locarno, behind the facade of public fellowship, was one of bitter confrontation between a fearful France flanked by the unhappy east Europeans, trying to hide their humiliation and panic, and a resentful, **revisionist** Germany demanding even more alterations in the power balance to her benefit. Since Germany was potentially the strongest power on the continent, the private fears of her neighbours could only deepen.
>
> Yet the public faces remained serene and smiling, and the ordinary European did not know about the clashes behind closed doors … The public facade of the Locarno conference and the treaties themselves had created an illusion of peace, and ordinary men rejoiced. Misled by a false front, Europe thankfully entered upon the Locarno years, thinking that real peace had arrived at last. Of all the interwar years these were perhaps the best years, but none the less they were years of illusion.

Just as contemporaries saw good reason for optimism, so historians, like Marks (with, it should be said, the benefit of hindsight), have seen good reason for pessimism. By 1931 Germany had secured substantial revision of the Treaty of Versailles. But most Germans were still not satisfied with Stresemann's achievements. Indeed, after his death in 1929, German statesmen abandoned Stresemann's conciliatory tone and adopted a more confrontational style. It was clear that future German governments, of whatever political complexion, were likely to seek further revision, especially in eastern Europe. The large vote for the Nazis in the 1930 German election did not auger well for the future.

There were also problems elsewhere. The situation in China was worrying. None of the various competing governments could long maintain much effective control. China's weakness was a constant temptation to Japan, which needed new markets and raw materials and still had imperial ambitions (see pages 69–72).

Praise or blame?

Many historians have criticised the British statesmen of the 1920s for their complacency and lack of foresight. Some condemn them for not supporting French efforts to maintain the Treaty of Versailles. Some argue that if Britain had given France the assurances of support that it sought, French policy towards Germany might not have been so intransigent. Others claim that

Britain should have offered more concessions to meet some of Germany's more reasonable complaints in the hope of consolidating the German 'moderates' in power.

However, it is possible to defend British policy. Even with the benefit of hindsight, historians cannot agree whether a consistent 'hard' or 'soft' approach to Germany would have been the more effective. In the circumstances British efforts to find a 'middle way' made sense. British statesmen appreciated French security fears, but did their best to appease Germany whenever possible. After the experience of the First World War it was only natural that Britain was determined to avoid entanglements, especially military obligations, on the Continent.

British policy-makers did not have a crystal ball. Very few people in the 1920s – not even Winston Churchill – foresaw the dark days ahead. Neither Germany, Italy nor Japan seemed to pose a particularly serious threat to world peace in 1930–1. Britain's relations with all three countries had been reasonably amicable throughout the 1920s. It is not easy to see, even now, what rational actions the politicians of the 1920s could have taken that would have prevented the threat of Hitler, Mussolini and the Japanese militarists in the 1930s. The great world-wide depression of the 1930s, which followed in the wake of the 1929 Wall Street Crash in the USA, came out of the blue. Few had predicted it. Fewer still could foresee its political repercussions and the effect they would have on British foreign policy.

Some key books in the debate

W.S. Churchill, *The Second World War: Vol. 1, The Gathering Storm* (Cassell, 1948).

P.W. Doerr, *British Foreign Policy, 1919–1939* (Manchester University Press, 1998).

S. Marks, *The Illusion of Peace: International Relations in Europe, 1918–1933* (Palgrave Macmillan, 2003).

A. Orde, *British Policy and European Reconstruction after the First World War* (Cambridge University Press, 1990).

Study Guide: Advanced Level Questions

In the style of Edexcel
Answer either question.
1. With what success did successive British governments seek to promote disarmament and international harmony during the 1920s? (60 marks)
2. To what extent did Britain seek to soften the impact of the Treaty of Versailles in its relations with Germany during the 1920s? (60 marks)

Exam tips

The cross-references are intended to take you straight to the material that will help you to answer the questions.

1. It is worth beginning by examining the situation in 1919. You will need to refer back to Chapter 2 (pages 16–28) for information about:
   - the scars left by the First World War
   - the outcome of the Versailles peace settlement.

   Assume that successive British governments did seek to promote disarmament and international harmony in the 1920s. However, you might indicate that Conservative and Labour governments did pursue different policies, not least with regard to the USSR. You will then need to decide how you will order your material. Disarmament policies should not be too difficult (pages 55–7). How successful were British policies? The pursuit of international harmony might be more challenging. You will need to examine each of the following areas:
   - the League of Nations (pages 53–5)
   - Britain's relations with Germany (pages 47–52)
   - Britain's relations with the USSR (pages 39–45)
   - Britain's relations with Italy (pages 45–7).

   It is important that you evaluate the success of British policies, in respect to international harmony, and that this evaluation pervades your answer and is not something simply bolted on at the end. Assess British success in each area that you examine. It may be that policy-making was more successful in some areas than others. Your conclusion should pull together your various, and maybe varied, assessments of British foreign policy in the 1920s.

2. Question 2 asks you to focus on British relations with Germany in the 1920s. In your introduction you will need to say something (in brief) about the Treaty of Versailles. You will then need to explore the issues of 'impact' and 'soften'. It is usually a good technique to give some indication of the line of your argument and your likely conclusion. Other paragraphs should consider the following questions:
   - What were the main terms of the Treaty of Versailles (pages 22–5)?
   - What were Germany's main grievances after 1919 (pages 26–7)?
   - To what extent did British governments sympathise with Germany post-1919 (pages 47–9)?
   - To what extent were British policies different from those of France (pages 47–52)?
   - What were the main areas of tension and debate in the 1920s (pages 58–60)?

   You will still need to write a concluding paragraph that draws together the major points you have made in order to give an overall judgement. Was much actually done to soften the impact of the Treaty of Versailles?

In the style of OCR

Study the following four passages A, B, C and D, about British attitudes towards Germany in the 1920s, and answer both of the sub-questions that follow.

Passage A

From: Richard Overy with Andrew Wheatcroft, The Road to War, *first published in 1989. Overy and Wheatcroft stress that Britain had a global rather than a European outlook.*

In practice Britain's commitment to collective security was always an ambiguous one. Though the belief in peace and international order was real enough, Britain took a global rather than a European view of its responsibilities. Britain's relationship with Europe, where collective security was most in demand, was, in the words of Austen Chamberlain, British Foreign Secretary under Baldwin, 'semi-detached'. Britain saw itself as a disinterested spectator of European affairs, a genial but aloof umpire, reasonable but not committed. 'For us', wrote Robert Vansittart at the Foreign Office, 'European politics are mostly other people's feuds and grievances … Beyond a certain point, the quarrels of Europe are not our quarrels …'. As a result Britain became increasingly isolated in the 1920s, returning to a diplomatic tradition which had been broken only by the growing world crisis before 1914. British politicians of all parties were reluctant to uphold the letter of the Treaty of Versailles, which many found unreasonable and vindictive. Relations with France cooled rapidly after 1919. There were no formal ties to any other major power. The one alliance Britain did have, the 1902 Treaty with Japan, was allowed to lapse in 1922. Though Britain remained a clear defender of the status quo, it did so on its own terms, independently.

Passage B

From: M. Pugh, The Making of Modern British Politics 1867–1939, *published in 1982. Pugh is a historian who argues that Labour and Conservative governments followed very similar policies towards Germany in the 1920s, policies which can best be described as limited appeasement and limited disarmament.*

In practice, Labour and Conservative governments operated a bi-partisan policy in the 1920s involving strictly limited steps towards the appeasement of German grievances – a downward revision of reparations, persuading the French to quit the Ruhr and an early evacuation of the Rhineland. Appeasement thus stopped well short of accepting the right to national unity of all Germans or of permitting Germany's re-establishment as a major military power. In spite of the impression of fundamental differences between the pacifist left and the Conservative right, the position of the Labour leaders closely approached that of Conservative and National governments. By 1922, expenditure on the armed forces had been cut back to £110 million – from

£600 million in 1920 – and remained around that level until 1935 when both parties decided rearmament was necessary.

Passage C

From: W.N. Medlicott, British Foreign Policy Since Versailles 1919–1963, first published in 1968. Medlicott is generally critical of British policymakers in the 1920s and thinks opportunities were missed.

Nevertheless, by 1931 the chance had been lost of retreating from the more impracticable League obligations with a good face. The same is perhaps true of Anglo-German relations; Austen Chamberlain's loyalty to France led him to acquiesce all too readily in their hostility to further concessions. The 'Locarno period' from 1925 to 1929 certainly brought about a noticeable amelioration in Germany's position. But grievances remained which could have been removed at this stage without loss of prestige. Even such steps as the cancellation of reparations, the return of the colonies, the revision by arbitration of Germany's eastern frontiers, might have been carried out before 1930 without any appearance of surrender to German aggression, and the effect would have been to strengthen the more liberal tendencies which were overwhelmed in the debacle of Germany's economic crisis between 1929 and 1933.

Passage D

From: C. Barnett, The Collapse of British Power, first published in 1972, a historian who argues that the British desire to appease Germany put Britain in a weak position throughout the 1920s and 1930s.

Appeasement was set in motion as early as Versailles, and then continued to be the theme of British policy towards Germany; appeasement in the sense of soothing and conciliating as well as bringing peace. By 1920, what was to be the enduring relationship between Britain and Germany between the wars had been established; Britain, though the victor, sought the consent of the vanquished; Germany, although defeated, was in the dominating position of having to give consent. And the more touchy and stand-offish Germany became, the more anxiously Britain sought her consent. It was an absurd reversal of what ought to have been. It yielded the initiative to Germany, enabling her to fight from the strongest position, strategically offensive, tactically defensive. This initiative was ruthlessly and successfully exploited by German governments from 1920 to 1938.

1. Using these four passages and your own knowledge, assess the view that British statesmen in the 1920s were complacent and lacking in foresight with regard to the problem of Germany. (30 marks)

2. Assess the view that British foreign policy in the period 1919–31 was successful in contributing to the peace and stability of Europe. (45 marks)

Exam tips

The cross-references are intended to take you straight to the material that will help you to answer the questions.

1. Remember that good answers will not deal with the issues in each passage but will arrange them thematically to create a more sophisticated answer (for example, 'A and D agree that … whereas B and C …'). You should aim to integrate your own knowledge, not least your understanding of the historical debate, with the passages so that together the proposition in the question is evaluated. Take note of just how much the introduction to each of the passages tells you about the contents. To what extent are the four passages critical of British statesmen? What policies do each of the passages think Britain adopted? You would do well to point out that the difference between the four accounts is often a subtle one. Try and decide which passage is nearest your own view of British policy-making in the 1920s. You can then use your own knowledge to suggest how helpful and reliable the passages are in providing an overview of British foreign policy. The key debate (pages 58–60) and the section on the German question (pages 47–51) should provide extra information and help your understanding of the question. Make your assessment in the light of what you already know.

2. It is worth mentioning in your introduction the problems facing British statesmen in the 1920s. It is also worth stressing that the 1920s was essentially a decade of peace and stability. To what extent did Britain contribute to this situation? Were British statesmen skilful or just lucky? Give some indication of your conclusion. You will need to have paragraphs on the following issues:
    *   To what extent did British power limit Britain's actions (pages 1–6)?
    *   What were Britain's main aims post-1919 (pages 11–14)?
    *   How successful was British policy towards Germany (pages 47–51)?
    *   How successful was British policy towards the USSR (pages 39–45)?
    *   Did Italy pose much of a threat (pages 45–7)?
    *   How successful was the League of Nations (pages 53–5)?
    *   How much was achieved on the disarmament front (pages 55–7)?

    Reach a conclusion that essentially sums up what you think and what you have already written. How much influence did Britain have in European affairs? Were British aims sensible? How successful was Britain in tackling the problems of Germany, the USSR and Italy? Was much done to promote the League of Nations and world disarmament? Did British statesmen achieve most of their aims? If so was this more by good luck than good judgement?

    Remember that evidence should be used in essay answers to evaluate the historical debate.

4

The Gathering Storm 1931–6

POINTS TO CONSIDER

Between 1931 and 1936 British governments faced problems with regard to Germany, Italy and Japan. British foreign policy in the early 1930s was criticised at the time (most notably by Winston Churchill) and has been criticised by historians since. The main charge is that Britain should have taken stronger action against the Japanese militarists, Mussolini and Hitler. This chapter will examine why British governments did not take a harder line, by focusing on the following themes:

- Depression and disarmament
- The problem of Japan 1931–3
- The problem of Germany 1933–5
- The problem of Italy 1935–6
- The Rhineland, Spain and rearmament

Key dates

1931	August	National Government formed in Britain
	September	Japanese troops began military operations in Manchuria
1932	February	Import Duties Act
	October	Lord Lytton's Commission reported on the Manchuria situation
1933	January	Hitler became German Chancellor
	October	Germany left the Disarmament Conference and the League of Nations
1935	March	Hitler announced German rearmament
	April	Stresa Front
	June	Anglo-German Naval Agreement
	October	Italy invaded Abyssinia
1936	March	German troops re-occupied the Rhineland
	July	Start of the Spanish Civil War

1| Depression and Disarmament

At the start of the 1930s, there seemed every chance that the peace and stability of the 1920s might continue. There were some problems but they did not seem particularly dangerous. Few people seriously contemplated the possibility of a major war. But from 1931 there were to be increasing threats to international peace. Many arose from the effects of the terrible world-wide economic depression that followed the 1929 **Wall Street Crash**.

The Great Depression

Britain was hit hard by the Depression. The coal, textiles, shipbuilding, and iron and steel industries were all badly affected. Trade fell by 40 per cent. By 1932 over 20 per cent of the British workforce was unemployed. The search for economic recovery eclipsed everything else, including foreign policy. Ramsay MacDonald's Labour government clung firmly to **orthodox economics**, cutting government spending and trying to balance the budget.

In 1931 a massive financial crisis loomed; confidence in sterling sagged and Britain was forced to come off the **Gold Standard**. The Labour Cabinet was divided on whether to cut money paid to the unemployed. In an effort to save the economy, MacDonald split the Labour Party and joined forces with the opposition in a National Government. In October 1931 a general election was called and the electors were asked to give the National Government a free hand to deal with the crisis situation.

The National Government gained the biggest majority in modern history: 554 MPs against 61 for all the other groups combined. The Conservatives won 473 seats – over 75 per cent of the House of Commons (and the last occasion to date on which a British government gained more than 50 per cent of the popular vote). The pattern of British politics had been massively altered. There was no credible alternative government. MacDonald remained Prime Minister, but the National Government was essentially Conservative and increasingly dominated by Stanley Baldwin, the Tory leader, and Neville Chamberlain, the Chancellor of the Exchequer.

Imperial preference

British leaders would have preferred international co-operation to bring about world economic recovery since Britain was so dependent on world trade. However, the Great Depression encouraged all countries to think primarily of themselves. In order to protect its own industries, Britain finally abandoned **free trade** and turned to **imperial preference**. The Import Duties Act of February 1932 imposed a 10 per cent tax on most imported goods, except those from the British Empire. The Ottawa Conference in July 1932 led to Britain and the Dominions agreeing to establish an imperial economic bloc, protecting their trade by a system of **tariffs** against countries outside the Commonwealth.

Key question
What impact did the Depression have on British foreign policy 1931–3?

Key terms

Wall Street Crash
In October 1929 share prices on the New York stock exchange (on Wall Street) collapsed. Many US banks and businesses lost money. This event is often seen as triggering the Great Depression.

Orthodox economics
The usual view of economic experts is that governments should only spend as much money as they receive from taxation.

Gold Standard
Sterling's value was fixed on the basis of its value in gold, with banks being obliged to exchange notes for gold coin. By coming off the Gold Standard in September 1931 the pound devalued against the US dollar.

Key dates

The National Government formed in Britain: August 1931

The Import Duties Act: February 1932

Key question
Why did Britain's hopes of disarmament not materialise?

Key terms

Free trade
The interchange of all commodities without import and export duties.

Imperial preference
Britain tried to ensure than countries within the Empire and Commonwealth traded first and foremost with each other.

Tariffs
Import duties.

Support for disarmament

The National Government, committed to restoring sound finances, was reluctant to maintain defence expenditure. Many, particularly on the left, saw no point in spending money on armaments, believing that they were more likely to cause a war than to prevent one. Indeed most Labour and Liberal politicians rejected the use of force as an instrument of policy, pressed for disarmament as the chief element in British foreign policy, and developed their opposition to the National Government mainly on this issue.

Throughout the 1920s there had been an increasing spate of anti-war literature – poems, plays and autobiographies – condemning the futility and wastefulness of the First World War. A host of anti-war organisations – the National Peace Council, the League of Nations Union and the Peace Pledge Union – sprang up and seemed to be gaining in strength. In October 1933 in the East Fulham by-election, a Conservative candidate who advocated an increase in defence spending was defeated by a pacifist Labour opponent. The Conservative majority of over 14,000 was transformed into a Labour majority of nearly 5000.

Even the public schools seemed to be turning out pacifists. In 1933 the Oxford Union resolved by 257 votes to 153 that 'this house will not fight for King and Country'.

The National Government, intending to ward off Labour and Liberal attacks, strongly adhered to the principles of disarmament and international co-operation through the League of Nations. Almost all politicians – Conservative, Labour and Liberal – regarded the League as an alternative to armaments. No-one believed in rearming in order to support the League of Nations. It was assumed that goodwill and enlightened opinion, plus the threat of economic sanctions, would deter potential aggressors.

The World Disarmament Conference

MacDonald pinned great hopes on the World Disarmament Conference, which met in Geneva in February 1932. Arthur Henderson, a Labour colleague and ex-British Foreign Secretary, was the conference president. The main problem from the start was Germany's claim for parity of treatment. Britain was prepared to accept this claim, but France, the strongest military power in Europe, still feared Germany, and French leaders were not prepared to reduce their forces without watertight guarantees of security. To France it seemed as if 'equality of rights' meant that Germany would be able to rearm and again threaten to attack them. It proved impossible to find a compromise between the German demand for equality and the French demand for security.

The situation in 1932–3

Despite failure on the disarmament front, MacDonald continued to hope that the just grievances of Germany could be settled by negotiation. Given Germany's dreadful economic position (over five million people unemployed in 1932), most British MPs felt that reparations should be cancelled. In June 1932 a conference under the presidency of MacDonald met at Lausanne in Switzerland. This conference succeeded in settling the reparations problem. Germany agreed to make a final payment of 2.6 million marks to a European Reconstruction Fund. In return German reparation payments would be abolished.

This was one of the last successes of the collective diplomacy that had prevailed for much of the 1920s. Collective diplomacy had tended to favour the maintenance of the status quo and thus had suited British interests. But in the early 1930s Britain's international position began to deteriorate rapidly. The world-wide depression had different effects in different countries. It made some countries, like the USA, more peaceful than ever. In others it undermined democracy and led to governments coming to power which favoured war and foreign conquest as a means of acquiring new lands, markets and raw materials to help alleviate the economic situation. As a result the international climate became increasingly threatening and Britain faced potential challenges from Japan, Germany and Italy. Trust in disarmament and collective security, and the consequent cutback in military spending, meant that Britain was not well prepared for the dangers that lay ahead.

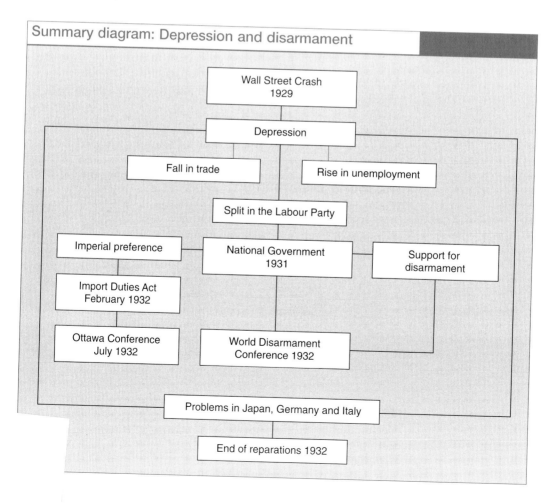

Summary diagram: Depression and disarmament

Key question
Why was Japan a problem?

Key date

Japanese troops began military operations in Manchuria: September 1931

Key term

Constitutional monarchy
Government where the powers of the monarch are defined and limited.

2 | The Problem of Japan

By the 1920s Japan was a major economic, military and imperial power. It had secured Formosa from China in 1895, Korea from Russia in 1905, and after 1914 had taken all German colonies in China and the Pacific north of the Equator. It also had substantial interests in Manchuria, a large province that it leased from China.

Japan was nominally a **constitutional monarchy**, under the Emperor Hirohito, and for most of the 1920s had been governed by a succession of liberal coalitions. Most of these governments supported international co-operation and favoured peaceful resolutions of conflicts between nations. But Japan had been disappointed by its gains from the First World War and favoured expansion. The turmoil in China and the often provocative policies of the Chinese government provided a permanent incitement to Japan to intervene.

The onset of the Great Depression at the start of the 1930s hit Japan hard and was a powerful incentive to military adventure. Territorial expansion could provide the raw materials and markets it lacked. A growing number of radical nationalists, especially strong in the army, wanted Japan to pursue its own national interests and not be constrained by the 'rules' of the West. Assassinations of politicians who opposed the nationalist cause became an increasingly common phenomenon.

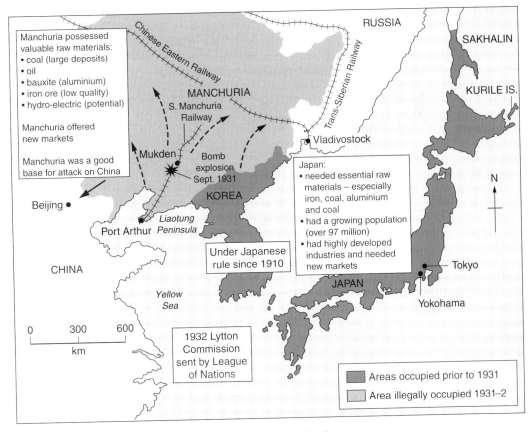

Figure 4.1: The Japanese occupation of Manchuria 1931–2.

Manchuria

In September 1931 units in the Japanese army, acting without orders from their government, seized a number of points in Manchuria (see Figure 4.1). Aware of popular support for the occupation of Manchuria, the Japanese government did little to halt the army. China immediately appealed to the League of Nations.

Japan's action was the first real challenge by a major power to the 'new international system' and there was concern that Article 16 of the Covenant of the League might be invoked. This article declared that if any member of the League should resort to war in disregard to its obligations, this would amount to an act of war against all other members of the League. The League was then empowered to subject the aggressor to immediate economic sanctions.

However, it was by no means clear that Japan had committed a 'resort to war' in an area where incidents between Chinese and Japanese soldiers were commonplace. Moreover, China did not immediately attempt to invoke Article 16 and so at first the League did little except appeal to China and Japan to refrain from action that might worsen the situation. But the Japanese army was in no mood to be coerced by verbal warnings from the League. By February 1932 it had occupied the whole of Manchuria and set up the puppet state of **Manchukuo**.

British reaction

Britain was concerned with the developments in Manchuria. It had major economic and political interests in the Far East – in Hong Kong, Malaya, Singapore and Shanghai – and a military presence in the area. Most British politicians were critical of Japan's action, particularly when Chinese forces were attacked near Shanghai, and the British government was certainly not prepared to recognise Manchukuo.

However, there was also some sympathy for Japan. Anglo-Japanese relations had been friendly for many years. Japan, like Britain, had suffered considerable provocation from Chinese nationalists throughout the 1920s. Much of China was in a state of political chaos. Japan had at least brought relative prosperity to the part of Manchuria it had previously controlled, might well restore order in the whole of Manchuria, and would certainly provide a bulwark against Bolshevik aggression.

Britain had more than enough domestic problems in 1931–2 and had no intention of risking a major war with Japan. British forces in the Far East were small and Singapore and Hong Kong were essentially undefended. Economic sanctions were unlikely to achieve much. The Royal Navy was not strong enough to enforce a trade embargo and the USA, Japan's biggest trading partner, made it clear it would not support any League action. As a result, main aim throughout the Manchurian crisis was to try to an agreement between Japan and China.

Key question
What action should Britain have taken?

Key date

Lord Lytton's
Commission reported
on the Manchuria
situation: October
1932

The Lytton Commission

The League of Nations set up a commission under Lord Lytton to look into the rights and wrongs of what had happened in Manchuria. Lytton spent many months in Manchuria and China before issuing his final report in October 1932. The Lytton Commission declared that many of the Japanese grievances were justified, but condemned Japan's methods of redressing those grievances. It recommended that Manchuria should have autonomous status under Chinese supervision. The League accepted Lytton's recommendations by 42 votes to 1. Japan, the only nation to vote against the recommendations, withdrew from the League in protest and ignored its rulings.

Key question
How troubled were
Anglo-Japanese
relations after 1932?

Anglo-Japanese relations 1932–7

Britain condemned Japan's action but did little else. Given its weak military position, there was much to be said for caution. If action was to be taken, US support was vital – but that support was not forthcoming. Japanese imperialism was a potential threat to British interests in the Far East, and possibly even to India, Australia and New Zealand. But it was not an immediate threat. Indeed Japanese expansion in northern China could be seen as reducing the risk of Japanese expansion in other, more sensitive, areas in Asia.

The best policy, therefore, seemed to be to accept Japan's take-over of Manchuria and to hope that the Japanese threat did not develop. A few limited precautions were taken. Work was resumed on the Singapore naval base and the so-called '10-Year Rule' (page 13), the diplomatic and military assumption that no major war would occur in the next 10 years, was abandoned. However, in practice, this meant very little. Britain did not yet embark on a serious programme of rearmament.

Some politicians, such as Neville Chamberlain, were keen to restore friendly relations with Japan as soon as possible, if needs be at the expense of China. This seemed a good way to protect British possessions and investments in the Far East. It might also reduce the amount of money that Britain would have to spend on improving her defences to combat Japan. But others realised that an Anglo-Japanese pact:

- would have little moral justification
- might further damage the prestige of the League of Nations
- would do untold damage to Britain's relations with China, the USSR and especially the USA. (Both the USA and the USSR distrusted Japan.)

Relations between Britain and Japan remained uneasy. Throughout the 1930s different military and political factions in Japan often pursued conflicting policies and Britain found it hard to accept that chaos and confusion, rather than duplicity, frequently lay behind the twists and turns of Japanese policy. But Japanese nationalists increasingly stressed that Japan regarded the whole of China and East Asia as its special sphere of influence. This was worrying. So was the fact that Japan made i clear that it intended to end the existing naval agreements and to increase its navy.

The **Anti-Comintern Pact**, signed by Germany and Japan in November 1936, further alarmed Britain. The Pact was aimed primarily against the USSR, but might be a potential threat to Britain. British efforts to bring about some kind of reconciliation between China and Japan failed. Nevertheless the British government had no wish to alienate Japan unnecessarily and relations between Britain and Japan did improve slightly in 1936 and early 1937.

Anti-Comintern Pact

A treaty between Germany and Japan (joined by Italy in 1937) in which they declared their common hostility to communism.

Key term

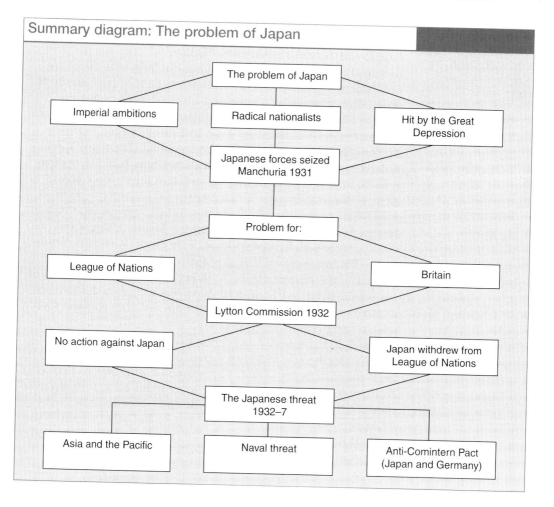

Summary diagram: The problem of Japan

- The problem of Japan
- Imperial ambitions
- Radical nationalists
- Hit by the Great Depression
- Japanese forces seized Manchuria 1931
- Problem for:
- League of Nations
- Britain
- Lytton Commission 1932
- No action against Japan
- Japan withdrew from League of Nations
- The Japanese threat 1932–7
- Asia and the Pacific
- Naval threat
- Anti-Comintern Pact (Japan and Germany)

3 | The Problem of Germany 1933–5

Adolf Hitler

In 1933 Adolf Hitler came to power in Germany. This was a cause for alarm – if not panic – in many countries, not least Britain. It ⟨c⟩ertain that Hitler's **Nazi** government would challenge ⟨ng⟩ European balance of power. But the exact nature of ⟨th⟩em was not easy to determine then, or now. Possible

Key question
To what extent was Hitler a threat in 1933?

Hitler became German Chancellor: January 1933

Key date

Key terms

Nazi
Short for National Socialist German Workers Party. It can also mean a supporter of Adolf Hitler.

Lebensraum
'Living space'. Hitler hoped to expand Germany's 'living space' in the east, at the expense of Poland and the USSR.

Key term

Hegemony
Leadership or predominant power.

Key date

Germany left the Disarmament Conference and the League of Nations: October 1933

solutions to the threat posed by Hitler were, therefore, even more difficult to define.

Hitler was clearly intent on freeing Germany from the shackles of the Versailles settlement. He wanted to see an end to the restrictions on Germany's rearmament and its right to remilitarise the Rhineland. He also favoured the inclusion within Germany of all the German-speaking people in Europe, especially the Austrians and the Germans in Czechoslovakia and Poland. In his book *Mein Kampf*, written in the mid-1920s, he had also talked about winning **lebensraum** in the east.

Was *Mein Kampf* an early folly or a blueprint for the future? Even assuming it was a blueprint, did Hitler actually pose a threat to Britain? In *Mein Kampf* he spoke of Britain as a potential ally of Germany. His main ambitions seemed to be in eastern not western Europe. His chief enemy seemed likely to be the USSR. The prospect of a Germano-Russian war was not necessarily a bad thing from a British point of view. At the very least a stronger Germany would be a useful bulwark against Russian or Communist expansion.

However, there were some Britons who feared the worst. Sir Robert Vansittart, the leading civil servant at the Foreign Office, warned ministers from the start about the threat of Nazism. So too did Winston Churchill. They were not alone. A report from the Defence Requirements Committee concluded in 1934 that, 'We take Germany as the ultimate potential enemy against whom our long-range defensive policy must be directed'.

But the fact that some people distrusted Hitler gave no-one the right or power to intervene in Germany. Some hoped, and indeed expected, that Hitler would not last long. If he failed to solve Germany's economic problems, he might well lose power. Many believed that Hitler might well become less extreme now he was German Chancellor. Some British observers thought there was a limit to his ambitions. They were convinced that he sought German equality rather than **hegemony** in Europe. There remained considerable sympathy for German grievances and many thought that greater efforts should be made to redress those grievances.

Fortunately there seemed to be no immediate German threat. It was assumed that it would take Hitler a long time to get Germany back on its feet. Some thought that Britain should help Germany's economic recovery. This was a view particularly supported by the Bank of England and the Board of Trade. There would be considerable economic gains for Britain if Germany again became prosperous. The return of German prosperity might also help to heal the wounds of the past and produce an atmosphere of international friendship and understanding.

Profile: Adolf Hitler 1889–1945

1889	– Born in Austria, the son of a customs official
1905	– Left school without qualifications
1907–8	– Failed to get into a Viennese art school
1908–13	– Lived as something of a down-and-out in Vienna
1913	– Moved to Munich in Bavaria, Germany, to evade conscription into the Austrian army
1914	– Joined a Bavarian regiment. During the First World War, he fought well, winning the Iron Cross for bravery. Amazingly, he never rose in rank beyond corporal
1919	– Joined the German Workers' Party as its 55th member
1921	– Became leader (or *Führer*) of the party, now known as the Nazi Party
1923	– Failed in his attempt to seize power in the Munich Beer Hall *Putsch*
1924	– Imprisoned for a year: used his time in prison to write *Mein Kampf* (*My Struggle*)
1930	– The Nazi Party became the second largest party in Germany
1932	– The Nazi Party became the single largest party in Germany
1933	– Hitler became Chancellor
1934	– On the death of President Hindenburg, Hitler became *Führer*
1935	– Announced German rearmament
1936	– German troops occupied the Rhineland
1938	– The *Anschluss*: Austria joined with Germany
	– The Munich Conference: Hitler won the Sudetenland from Czechoslovakia
1939	– Germany effectively took over the rest of Czechoslovakia
	– Germany invaded Poland, triggering the Second World War
1940	– German forces overran Denmark, Norway, the Netherlands, Belgium and France: Hitler controlled virtually all Europe except Britain and the USSR
1941	– Operation Barbarossa: Hitler invaded the USSR
	– Hitler declared war on the USA
1942–3	– German forces defeated at Stalingrad in the USSR
1944	– D-Day: Allied forces invaded France
1945	– Hitler committed suicide in Berlin

Historians continue to disagree about Hitler's ultimate intentions. In 1961 A.J.P. Taylor, in his book *The Origins of the Second World War*, claimed that Hitler was really a rather ordinary German statesman with a rather ordinary mission – that of increasing Germany's standing among the world's nations. He was, said Taylor, no different to previous German leaders. He was a man who took advantage of situations as they arose and rarely took the initiative himself. He was no more wicked or unscrupulous than most other statesmen.

A.J.P. Taylor was often prone to overstatement and his book sparked off a great and, at times, bitter debate among historians. Few historians today accept Taylor's arguments in their entirety. Most probably think that Hitler had a clear and cold-blooded general purpose to:

- overthrow the Treaty of Versailles
- win *lebensraum* in eastern Europe
- make Germany the strongest power in Europe.

However many now accept that Hitler had no detailed programme but simply improvised as events unfolded. Given the debates among historians about Hitler's objectives, it is hardly surprising that British politicians in the 1930s were unsure about how to deal with the new German leader.

Hitler's first moves 1933–4

Key question
How serious a threat
was Hitler in 1933–4?

Hitler's first moves in foreign policy were relatively cautious. He certainly did not seem particularly hostile to Britain. He gave several interviews to British journalists and went out of his way to express admiration for Britain and its Empire and to voice the hope that 'the two great Germanic nations' could work together.

However, in October 1933 Germany withdrew from both the Disarmament Conference at Geneva (page 67) and the League of Nations. Hitler's justification was that the great powers would not treat Germany as an equal. This action effectively destroyed the Disarmament Conference. Without German participation, no useful agreement could be reached. Yet a long time would elapse before enthusiasts could admit to themselves that the Disarmament Conference was dead. Many hoped that Hitler might be persuaded to return it.

In 1933–4 most British MPs were aware that Germany was secretly rearming and thus becoming an increasing threat. In March 1934 Winston Churchill said in the House of Commons:

> Our nearest neighbour Germany is arming fast and no one is going to stop her. That seems quite clear. No one proposes a preventive war to stop Germany breaking the Treaty of Versailles. She is going to arm; she is doing it; she has been doing it. I have no knowledge of the details, but it is well known that those very gifted people with their science and with their factories ... are capable of developing with great rapidity the most powerful Air Force for all purposes, offensive and defensive, within a very short period of time. I dread the day when the means of threatening the heart of the British Empire should pass into the hands of the present rulers of Germany ... No nation playing the part we play and aspire to play in the world has a right to be in a position where it can be blackmailed.

"WELL – WHAT ARE YOU GOING TO DO ABOUT IT NOW?"

'Well – What are you going to do about it now?' (a David Low cartoon). Shows from left to right, Simon, Mussolini, Daladier and Hitler. Sir John Simon was British Foreign Secretary. Daladier was French Minister of War and Defence. Mussolini was the fascist ruler of Italy. How has the cartoonist represented (a) Hitler and (b) the League of Nations? (David Low, *Evening Standard*, 2 October 1933, Centre for the Study of Cartoons and Caricature, University of Kent.)

Sir John Simon, the Foreign Secretary, admitted that:

> German civil aviation is now the first in Europe. Germany already has in effect a fleet of 600 military aeroplanes and facilities for its very rapid expansion. She can already mobilise an army three times as great as that authorised by the Treaty and a rapid expansion of her mobilisation facilities must be expected.

Prime Minister Stanley Baldwin was pessimistic:

> I think it is well for the man in the street to realise that there is no power on earth that can protect him from being bombed. Whatever people may tell him, the bomber will always get through. The only defence is offence, which means that you have to kill more women and children more quickly than the enemy if you want to save yourselves. I just mention that so that people may realise what is waiting for them when the next war comes.

In 1934 Britain began to spend more money on the RAF. But few people in Britain as yet feared war. Indeed the Labour Party strongly censured the government for increasing spending on defence and thus 'jeopardising the prospects of international disarmament'. Nor did Britain draw nearer to France. The British Cabinet, still suspicious of French intentions, was not prepared to support Anglo-French **staff talks**. The French, meanwhile, began to push ahead with the building of the Maginot Line, the great line of defences down their border with Germany.

Staff talks
Discussions held by military leaders.

Key term

The 1934 German–Polish Pact

Hitler continued to be cautious. In 1934, to the surprise of many of his own followers, he signed a non-aggression pact with Poland (previously regarded as Germany's arch-enemy).

Key terms

Putsch
An attempt to seize power, usually by force.

Conscription
Compulsory enrolment for military service.

Key dates

Hitler announced German rearmament: March 1935

Stresa Front: April 1935

Anglo-German Naval Agreement: June 1935

The 1934 Austrian *putsch*

A Nazi-inspired *putsch* in Austria in 1934 led to the assassination of the Austrian Chancellor, Dollfuss. Mussolini regarded Austria as an Italian satellite state and rushed 100,000 Italian troops to the Austrian border as a warning in case Hitler tried to take advantage of the confusion in Vienna. Mussolini's action enabled the Austrian authorities to stabilise the internal situation. Hitler did nothing to help the Austrian Nazis and their *putsch* failed.

Germany rearms

In March 1935 Hitler admitted that Germany had an air force and announced the introduction of **conscription**, forbidden under the terms of the Treaty of Versailles. The German army would be increased to about 500,000 men – five times the permitted number. Although everyone was aware that Germany had been violating the military clauses of Versailles for many years, Hitler's announcement was a diplomatic challenge that could not be ignored.

The heads of government and foreign ministers of Britain, France and Italy met at Stresa in Italy in April 1935. They condemned Hitler's action and resolved to maintain the existing treaty settlement of Europe and to resist any future attempt to change it by force. This agreement was known as the Stresa Front.

France also strengthened its ties with the USSR. In May 1935 France and the Soviet Union concluded a treaty of mutual assistance, although ratification was postponed for some time. This was reinforced by a Soviet–Czechoslovakian agreement. It seemed as though Europe intended to stand firm against the German threat.

Key question
Was the Anglo-German Naval Agreement a mistake?

The Anglo-German Naval Agreement

Britain still did not consider itself to be particularly threatened by Hitler, who so far had said nothing about naval rearmament. In June 1935 Britain signed a naval agreement with Germany. By the terms of this agreement, Germany was to have the right to build up to 35 per cent of Britain's capital ships and to be allowed parity in submarines. This agreement, signed without prior discussion with France or Italy, damaged the Stresa Front. Britain, by sanctioning a much larger German navy than was permitted by the Treaty of Versailles, seemed to be condoning Germany's rearmament immediately after the Stresa Front's condemnation of it.

Although the Anglo-German Naval Agreement was criticised by some at the time, and by many historians since, in 1935 it had the approval of the Admiralty, Foreign Office and the entire Cabinet. They thought the Naval Agreement was a realistic contribution to peace. The Geneva Disarmament Conference had failed, largely through French stubbornness. Many British politicians were angry at France's flirtation with Russia. The French seemed to be doing their best to encircle Germany with allies, a move that might encourage rather than avert war. Moreover Britain, which still imported half its required foodstuffs, was anxious about its navy. Given the Japanese threat in the Far East, the British government had no wish to face a greater danger in home waters. The agreement at least ensured that Britain maintained, and Germany accepted, a naval superiority twice as great as in 1914.

Hitler seems to have hoped that the agreement would lead to a fully fledged alliance with Britain. However, it was clear that British public opinion would accept nothing in the nature of an Anglo-German alliance. The Nazi dictatorship was unpopular in many quarters in Britain, especially on the left. But it was also clear that British public opinion would not approve using military force to overthrow Hitler. Germany now embarked on a rapid rearmament programme. This meant that henceforward Hitler could not be stopped without the risk of a major war.

Summary diagram: The problem of Germany

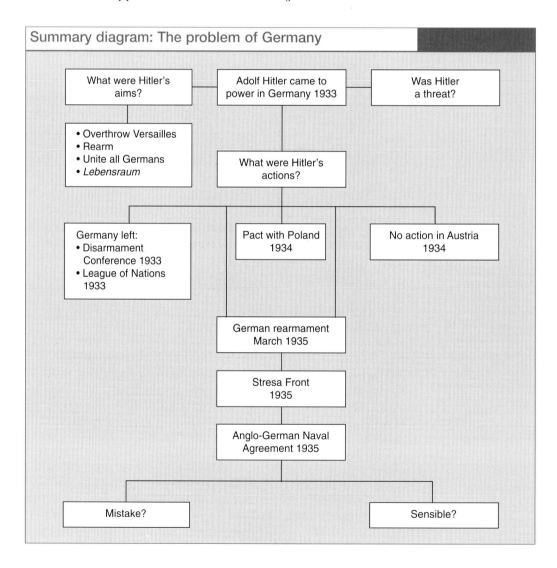

4 | The Problem of Italy 1935–6

Key question
How good were
Anglo-Italian relations
pre-1935?

Before 1935 relations between Italy and Britain had been reasonably satisfactory. However, Mussolini's ambitions to build up an empire in Africa and make the Mediterranean an 'Italian lake' meant that there was certainly potential for Anglo-Italian rivalry. Britain had its own colonial interests in Africa, and the Mediterranean was seen as essential to British trade routes. In the early 1930s there was increasing trouble between Britain and Italy in the Red Sea, Libya and Egypt. The fact that Mussolini, like many Italians, felt that Italy had made inadequate gains in the First World War was also a potential problem. Italy saw itself as a **'have-not' power** rather than a power committed to the preservation of the status quo. But for most of the 1920s and early 1930s Mussolini had done little to upset things and had generally sought prestige by remaining within the bounds of international society. In 1933 Britain saw Italy, along with France and the USA, as a friendly power against whom no major defence preparations were necessary.

Key term
'Have-not' power
A country that had not benefited from the Versailles peace settlement.

Indeed many British and French politicians hoped that Mussolini might be a useful ally against Hitler. There was some basis for these hopes. Mussolini had met Hitler in 1934 and had not been impressed. Italy was every bit as anxious as France about what would happen if Germany once again became a major power in central Europe. In particular, the prospect of a union between Germany and Austria, which would result in a powerful German state along Italy's northern border, terrified Italy. Mussolini's swift action in sending troops to the Austrian border in 1934 had done more than anything to stop Hitler intervening in Austria on the side of the Austrian Nazis. In April 1935 Italy had joined with France and Britain in the Stresa Front (page 77).

The problem of Abyssinia

Key date
Italy invaded
Abyssinia: October
1935

However, by 1935 trouble was brewing. Mussolini wanted to increase the Italian Empire in Africa by taking over Abyssinia (now known as Ethiopia), one of the last countries in Africa that was free from European control. Italy had long had designs on the region. In 1896 an Italian army had been defeated at Adowa by the Abyssinians and all Italian prisoners had been castrated. Many Italians still wanted to avenge this humiliating defeat.

In the early 1930s there were a number of incidents along the borders of Abyssinia and Italian Somaliland and Eritrea. As early as 1932 Italy began to make plans to take over Abyssinia. Mussolini believed that Italy needed more raw materials and living space for its rising population. Moreover, a bold foreign policy might be a useful distraction from economic distress in Italy. In 1934 there was a skirmish between Italian and Abyssinia forces at the border waterholes at Wal Wal. This incident was not staged by Mussolini, but it gave him a convenient excuse to build up his forces and prepare for an attack in October 1935.

Figure 4.2: Italy and its empire in 1939.

Diplomatic efforts to avert the Abyssinian crisis

Mussolini recognised that any advance in Africa might damage Italian relations with Britain and France. Therefore, he made considerable diplomatic efforts to ensure that they would accept his Abyssinian adventure. In January 1935 Laval, the French Foreign Minister, visited Rome and in effect promised Mussolini a free hand in Abyssinia. The French were very anxious to keep on good terms with Italy because of the increasing German threat. It also seemed that Britain was prepared to accept Italian expansion. The British were well aware of the Italian military build-up in Africa and yet no 'formal' mention of Abyssinia occurred at the Stresa Front in April 1935. Britain's silence, in Mussolini's view, implied consent.

However as the summer progressed, Britain made it clear that it would not approve of Italian annexation of the whole of Abyssinia. Britain's hostile reaction surprised and then angered Mussolini, but he determined to go through with his plan. Throughout the summer the world was presented with the spectacle of a crisis in slow motion. It was clear that Italy was planning a major invasion in the autumn when the rainy season ended. Attempts were made to reach a compromise settlement but with no success.

‘The awful warning’: a *Punch* cartoon (August 1935). What point was the cartoonist trying to make?

Baldwin becomes Prime Minister

In June 1935 the Conservative leader, Stanley Baldwin, replaced MacDonald as Prime Minister. Sir Samuel Hoare became Foreign Secretary and Anthony Eden entered the Cabinet as Minister for League of Nations Affairs. Baldwin had little interest in foreign policy and Hoare had relatively little experience. This may have given top civil servants like Sir Robert Vansittart more influence than usual. Vansittart considered Germany the main threat to Britain and in consequence was keen to appease Italy. On balance, however, the change of government made very little difference to British policy.

War!

Continued efforts were made to reach a compromise by offering Mussolini parts of Abyssinian territory. The Abyssinian Emperor, Haile Selassie, was prepared to accept some loss of land, but Mussolini was not satisfied with what he was offered. In October 1935 Italy invaded Abyssinia.

British reaction to the Abyssinian war

Haile Selassie immediately appealed to the League of Nations. Britain and France were now faced with a terrible choice. Haile Selassie was hardly a model ruler and Abyssinia was hardly a good neighbour. Abyssinia had caused Britain as much trouble on the Sudanese frontier as Italy had experienced on the Eritrean frontier. Britain, ironically, had unsuccessfully opposed Abyssinia's entry into the League of Nations in 1923. Neither Britain nor France had any real interests in Abyssinia. To take action, whether economic or military, against Mussolini would wreck the Stresa Front and, even worse, might force Italy into an agreement with Hitler.

Serious principles were at stake. The main one was whether Britain should honour its obligations under the League covenant (see page 53). Public opinion in Britain was strongly opposed to the Italian invasion. The results of the so-called **Peace Ballot**, held in 1934 but not declared until June 1935, showed considerable popular support for the League. Over 11.5 million people had voted in the ballot; 95 per cent thought Britain should remain in the League and large majorities had voted in favour of supporting economic and, if necessary, military measures against aggressor states. Public opinion could not be ignored, if only because a general election was in the offing.

Despite its previous readiness to consider concessions, the British government now took a moral stand. It condemned the Italian invasion and supported the League of Nations' action against Italy. The French government, anxious not to drive Mussolini into the German camp, but more anxious to keep in step with Britain, did likewise.

League of Nations action

In October 1935 the League denounced Italy as the aggressor and imposed economic sanctions. All imports from Italy and some exports were banned by virtually all members of the League. Seventy per cent of Italy's trade was with League members and it was assumed that economic pressure would bring Italy to a negotiated settlement.

The 1935 general election

In October Baldwin announced a general election. The National Government's sanctions policy, which avoided war, was popular and thus neatly tailored to the requirements of the election campaign.

As far as foreign policy was concerned, both Labour and the National Government said much the same thing; both committed themselves to the principle of collective security and both talked in general terms of the benefits of disarmament. Baldwin, although promising to 'remedy the deficiencies which have occurred in our defences', refused to emphasise new rearmament plans for fear of losing support.

With the economy improving and Baldwin inspiring calm, the National Government won a handsome victory, polling

Key question
What action should Britain have taken following the Italian invasion of Abyssinia?

Peace Ballot
A vote, held at the behest of the League of Nations Union in 1934, to test British support for the League.

Key term

Baldwin (right) with Sir Samuel Hoare after receiving the results of the Peace Ballot, July 1935.

11.8 million votes and winning 432 seats. Labour polled 8.3 million votes, winning 154 seats. The Liberals won 20 seats and the Communists one.

The Hoare–Laval Pact

Key question
Was the Hoare–Laval Pact a sensible solution to the crisis?

By early December most members of the League, headed by Britain and France, were applying a trade embargo against Italy. But the sanctions, which did not include an oil embargo, had limited effect on the Italian war effort. If anything they simply united the Italian people behind Mussolini. Closure of the **Suez Canal** might have been an even better way of damaging the Italian war effort than oil sanctions, but this might have led Mussolini to the 'mad dog act' of declaring war on Britain. The British government had no wish for a war against Italy, from which only Japan and Germany could benefit.

In December 1935 the British and French Foreign Ministers, Hoare and Laval, met in Paris to discuss the Abyssinian situation. They decided to propose a compromise settlement. Italy would receive about one-third of Abyssinia; in return Haile Selassie would remain Emperor and would be ceded a strip of Italian territory, giving Abyssinia access to the Red Sea. The British Cabinet approved the plan and Mussolini was ready to agree to it. However, when details of the so-called Hoare–Laval Pact were leaked to the press, there was a storm of indignation, not least

Key term

Suez Canal
The canal, which ran through Egyptian territory, joined the Mediterranean to the Red Sea. It was controlled by Britain.

among Conservative MPs, who felt the government was breaking its election promises and betraying its commitment to the League. In the face of this outburst, the Cabinet decided to abandon the Hoare–Laval Pact.

Hoare took most of the blame and resigned. In his resignation speech he said he had no regrets and claimed that his policy offered the best solution that Abyssinia could now hope for. However, Eden, the new Foreign Secretary, disliked and distrusted Mussolini and thought Britain should stand firm and support the League. In March 1936 Britain voted for oil sanctions, but refused to impose a full-scale naval blockade, and oil from the USA continued to flow into Italy. Nothing more was done to make sanctions bite.

The results of the Abyssinian war

Key question
What were the main consequences of the Abyssinian war?

Meanwhile the Italians fought well. In May 1936 Haile Selassie fled and Abyssinia became part of the Italian Empire. Mussolini's prestige in Italy soared. He boasted that 'the greatest colonial war in all history was the foundation stone of a new Roman Empire'.

In June 1936 Chancellor of the Exchequer Neville Chamberlain described the continuation of sanctions as the 'very midsummer of madness'. A week later the sanctions were withdrawn by Britain and the League. Chamberlain, like several other Cabinet members, had favoured a compromise solution throughout the crisis and was prepared to forgive Italian 'crimes' in the hope that Anglo-Italian friendship could be restored. But Britain continued to refuse to recognise the Italian conquest. This infuriated Mussolini and did Abyssinia little good.

The Abyssinian crisis had several important results:

- It was a death blow to the League of Nations, which had again failed to deter or halt an aggressor. This was a great shock to British public opinion. Collective security and the League, those concepts that had seemingly guarded British and world peace without the necessity to spend vast sums on armaments, had failed.
- The crisis had caused a major split between Italy and Britain and France. Mussolini felt bitter at the way he had been treated by the Western powers.
- Although Mussolini still regarded Hitler with some suspicion, he began to move closer to the German dictator who had consistently supported Italy's actions in Abyssinia.

Some historians have accepted Churchill's view, that the failure to check Mussolini in 1935–6 was an important step on the way to world war. Arguably Britain and the League should have been prepared to fight Mussolini. The assumption is that Italy would have been easily defeated and that this would have strengthened collective security and helped to deter later German aggression. But recently this argument has been questioned. Almost certainly Britain would have won a war against Italy; but victory would have left an embittered Italy and might not have been as easy as many have assumed. Italy was reasonably well prepared for war in

1935–6, unlike Britain. Moreover, Britain could scarcely have afforded the losses it was likely to sustain in even a successful war.

However, most historians are agreed that British policy in 1935–6 was weak and inept. It fell between two stools: the search for a compromise with Italy on the one hand, and the need to stand firm against Italian aggression on the other. In the end nothing had been achieved. Britain had failed either to uphold collective security or to appease Mussolini. To make matters worse, the Abyssinian crisis had revealed serious divisions between Britain and France.

Hitler was not slow to appreciate this weakness and division. He was also able to use the Abyssinian crisis for his next great gamble.

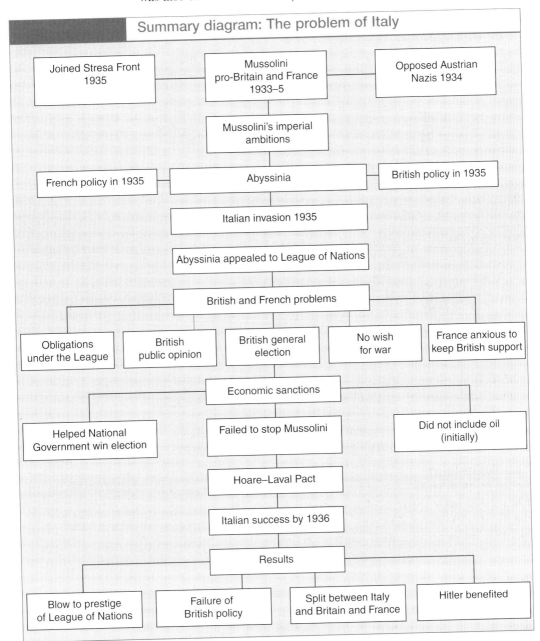

Summary diagram: The problem of Italy

5 | The Rhineland, Spain and Rearmament

Table 4.1: The gathering storm 1931–6: summary

Year	Britain	Germany	Italy	Japan	World
1931	National Government replaced Labour Government	Weimar Republic	Mussolini and fascists in power	Liberal politicians – challenged by army and radical Nationalists Manchuria	World-wide depression
1932	Ottawa Conference Imperial protection	Lausanne Conference The end of reparations	Plans for Abyssinian invasion	Manchukuo set up Lytton Commission	Depression continues World Disarmament Conference
1933		Hitler came to power Germany left League of Nations and World Disarmament Conference		Japan left the League of Nations	
1934	Peace Ballot	Non-aggression pact with Poland	Stopped Nazi *putsch* in Austria		
1935	Baldwin replaced MacDonald as Prime Minister Hoare–Laval Pact	Re-introduced conscription Anglo-German Naval Agreement	Stresa Front Invasion of Abyssinia		Franco-Russian treaty League of Nations imposed sanctions on Italy
1936	Four-year Rearmament Plan	Remilitarisation of Rhineland	Abyssinia became part of Italian Empire Rome–Berlin Axis	Anti-Comintern Pact with Germany	Spanish Civil War

The Rhineland

In March 1936 Hitler sent German troops into the demilitarised **Rhineland**, in clear violation of both the Treaty of Versailles and the Treaty of Locarno (see page 51), freely accepted by Germany in 1925. Hitler's justification was the ratification by the French

> **Key question**
> Should Britain have taken action against Hitler in 1936?

Key date

German troops re-occupied the Rhineland: March 1936

Senate of the 1935 Franco-Soviet alliance (see page 77), which he claimed was a threat to Germany. Hitler knew he was taking a considerable gamble. Germany was not strong enough to fight a long war and the token German forces that marched into the Rhineland had orders to withdraw at the first sign of French opposition.

Britain and France's reaction

Neither the French nor British government had been altogether surprised by Hitler's action. Both had expected that Hitler would raise the issue of the Rhineland as a topic for negotiation and both had a number of prior warnings from their intelligence staffs about the German move. Unlike the British, the French had the forces available to take action, but the fact that there was a **'caretaker' government** in France made a French call to arms unlikely. In the event, the French government did nothing, except pass the problem to Britain by asking if it would support French action.

The British government made it clear that it had no intention of risking war against Germany. Most British opinion saw Hitler's move into the Rhineland as regrettable in manner but not particularly threatening in substance. Most MPs probably agreed with Lord Lothian's remark that Germany had every right to walk into its own backyard. Some French politicians later claimed that France did not take action because Britain failed to offer support. However, it now seems certain that there was no will in France to risk war with or without British support.

The consequences of Hitler's action

Hitler had once again gambled and won. His troops remained in the Rhineland and began to build fortifications along the French frontier. Henceforward it would be even more difficult for Britain or France to take action against Germany.

In retrospect, many historians have claimed that Germany's march into the Rhineland offered 'the last chance' to stop Hitler without war, and thus the point at which he could and should have been challenged. It is possible that the threat of force might have led him to back down and that he might, as a consequence, have suffered a disastrous blow to his prestige. However, it was far from clear to French leaders at the time that Hitler would have pulled out of the Rhineland, and some historians have questioned the long-held view that he would have retreated if France and Britain had stood firm. In 1936 Germany might not have been the easy push-over that many historians have assumed. Certainly there was little that Britain could have done immediately to help France.

Only a few British politicians, most notably Churchill, pressed for a resolute stand against Germany. Most MPs thought that there was still insufficient evidence to suggest that Hitler's ambitions were entirely open-ended and violent. Anthony Eden, for example, believed that there might be much to be gained by accepting the German move and taking seriously Hitler's new

Key terms

Rhineland
The part of Germany to the west of the River Rhine. According to the Treaty of Versailles, it was to be permanently demilitarised.

Caretaker government
A temporary government. The French political situation was highly unstable. The country was seriously divided between right and left. Coalitions of various parties formed governments but then quickly fell out. The result was weak government.

proposals for a 25-year non-aggression pact. Through the summer of 1936 attempts were made to reach a stronger Anglo-German agreement. These attempts failed, but at least Britain and Germany remained on reasonably good terms throughout most of 1936–7. Hitler declared that he had no territorial claims in Europe, and for nearly two years he maintained a remarkably low profile. Germany continued to rearm, but not on the scale that many in the West later believed.

The Spanish Civil War

In July 1936 the attention of most British statesmen changed from Germany to Spain. Right-wing nationalists, led by General Franco and supported by **monarchists**, the Catholic Church and most of the armed forces, tried to overthrow the **Republican government**. The Republican government, supported by the industrial working class, liberals, socialists and communists, fought back.

British public opinion was excited and divided by the Spanish Civil War. The Labour Party and the left saw Franco as a fascist 'puppet', controlled by Mussolini and Hitler, and strongly supported the Republicans. About 2000 people from Britain went to Spain to join the **International Brigade** and fight against Franco, convinced that they were waging war against fascism. However, others sympathised with the Nationalists, saw the Republicans as essentially communist inspired, and some even went to fight on Franco's side.

The British government had little sympathy for either side in the civil war. Britain's main aim was to prevent the war spreading and becoming a general European conflict between the great powers. Therefore the government supported the setting up of a Non-Intervention Committee to discourage intervention on either side and enforce a ban on the export of war materials to Spain. Significantly the League of Nations was largely ignored. Most of the powers joined the committee but it was soon clear that its decisions were being flouted by Italy, Germany and Russia.

Mussolini supplied aircraft, armaments and nearly 100,000 men to help the Nationalists. Italian submarines sank merchant ships suspected of trading with the Republicans. Germany sent far fewer men, but used the war to test the value of new weapons and military techniques. The destruction of the small town of Guernica by German bombers in April 1937 made a great impression on contemporaries. The USSR sent men and weapons in an effort to help the communists on the Republican side. Spain, therefore, was transformed into a battleground of rival ideologies – the forces of communism against the forces of fascism.

The impact of the Spanish Civil War

The civil war dragged on for three bloody years. British fears that it might lead to a general war proved to be unfounded. Crises occurred, but in each case agreements were cobbled together.

Key question
What were the consequences of the Spanish Civil War?

Key date

Start of the Spanish Civil War: July 1936

Key terms

Monarchists
In terms of Spain, those who supported the return of a Spanish king.

Republican government
A left-wing government had been elected in 1936. The government seemed set to introduce a variety of radical reforms, which would reduce the power of the Catholic Church, big business and great landowners.

International Brigade
A left-wing military force made up of volunteers from a number of different countries.

Key term

Rome–Berlin Axis
A term first used by Mussolini in November 1936 to describe Italy's relationship with Germany. He envisaged European affairs being determined by, or revolving around, Italy and Germany.

However, many people in Britain were convinced that should a general war occur, the line-up would be on ideological grounds, rather than on the basis of perceived 'national interest'. Many on the left thought Britain should align itself on the anti-fascist side. Many on the right, on the other hand, while having little time for fascism, had no wish to align themselves with socialists and communists. Conservative opinion, on the whole, thought it was in Britain's best interest to stay out of any future ideological conflict.

Germany probably benefited most from the Spanish Civil War. Not only did it give Hitler an opportunity to test his new weapons, but it led to improved relations with Italy. In November 1936 Mussolini proclaimed the **Rome–Berlin Axis**. In 1937 Italy joined Germany and Japan in the Anti-Comintern Pact (see page 72). Relations between Britain and Italy sank to a new low.

Key question
How effective was British rearmament?

Rearmament

By the end of 1936 Britain faced serious problems:

- Germany was rearming
- Italy was a potential threat in the Mediterranean
- Japan had a substantial navy in the Far East
- The diplomatic outlook was not hopeful. The League of Nations was defunct and Britain had few strong, reliable allies.

In the circumstances Britain seemed to have little alternative but to rearm. The National Government was still hesitant. Additional military spending meant sacrificing other, more popular, programmes, housing, health or education. But already in 1935 a Defence White Paper had concluded that, 'Additional expenditure on the armaments of the three Defence Services can no longer be postponed'. In 1936 a Minister for the Co-ordination of Defence was appointed. Churchill would have loved the job, but it was given to Sir Thomas Inskip, a lawyer with no previous experience of the armed forces. Lord Cherwell, one of Churchill's friends, remarked that Inskip's appointment was 'the most cynical thing that has been done since Caligula appointed his horse a consul'.

In 1936 Neville Chamberlain introduced an extensive four-year plan for rearmament. This provided the framework for the military structure with which Britain entered the war in 1939. To help pay for it he placed a tax on tea, which was widely denounced as an attack on working class living standards. The increased rearmament was deplored by the Labour Party. The government was accused of rearming on 'a gigantic scale' and with too great haste. Most Labour MPs continued to oppose every major initiative for increased defence funding, right through to the introduction of conscription in 1939.

Table 4.2: Percentage of gross national product devoted to defence

Year	Germany	Britain
1933	1.0	3.0
1934	3.0	3.0
1935	7.4	3.3
1936	12.4	4.2
1937	11.8	5.6
1938	16.6	8.1
1939	23.0	21.4

Problems of rearmament

One of Britain's main problems was that it had to prepare for several different types of war. Britain had to be ready to fight a **colonial war**, a naval war in the Far East and a great European war. The nightmare scenario was that she might have to fight all three potential enemies – Germany, Italy and Japan – at the same time. Priority was naturally given to those services that could defend Britain from attack. Naval strength was essential to defend vital trade routes. Air defences were also a major concern. Far less money was spent on the army. Building bombers was seen as a cheaper and better way of preventing war in Europe than spending vast sums on building a large army. The assumption was that a major aerial bombing threat was likely to deter a hostile power from risking war with Britain.

Given the possibility of a long **war of attrition**, the government began to stockpile strategic materials (for example, oil) and make detailed plans for economic mobilisation. Much of this important economic preparation for war was hidden from the public.

More money could, and perhaps should, have been spent on rearmament, as Churchill claimed at the time and later. But the Treasury advised caution. Treasury officials and military experts realised that economic strength was as vital as having a powerful army, navy and air force. Unfortunately, Britain was short of machine tools and skilled labour. Up to one-sixth of the 1937 arms programme had to be met from imports. Increased military spending meant running the risk of a serious balance of payments crisis. This would undermine Britain's ability to continue importing for rearmament. Those, like Churchill, who argued in favour of more defence spending, ignored Britain's industrial weakness. The gradual expansion of forces, which avoided the temptation to spend large sums of money on weapons that would soon be outdated, also made sense. Given that there was no 'quick fix' to Britain's military weakness, it also made sense to buy time and reduce tension by diplomatic means.

Key terms

Colonial war
An overseas conflict in defence of Britain's imperial interests. It could be action against insurgents seeking independence or war against a hostile power.

War of attrition
A long conflict, in which both sides try to use their resources to wear down the enemy.

Conclusion

It is easy to criticise Britain for not taking action against Japan (in 1931–2), against Italy (in 1935–6) and against Germany (in 1936). But intervention on each occasion would probably have meant war – a war for which Britain was woefully unprepared militarily, economically, politically and psychologically. Few Britons at the time shared Churchill's enthusiasm for war. Of course, it is easy to be wise after the event. But were crucial British interests really at stake in Manchuria, in Abyssinia and in the Rhineland?

Summary diagram: The Rhineland, Spain and rearmament

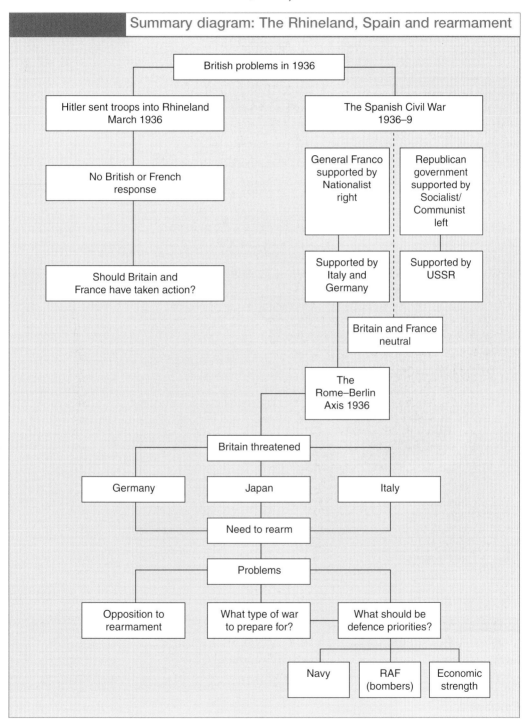

Study Guide: Advanced Level Questions

In the style of Edexcel

'In the light of what was known at the time, Britain's policy towards Germany in the period 1933 to 1936 was entirely sensible and understandable'. How far do you agree with this opinion? (60 marks)

Exam tips

The cross-references are intended to take you straight to the material that will help you to answer the questions.

You will first need to write an introduction. What were the main features of British policy towards Germany in the period? Presumably you will be stressing that Britain essentially tried to avoid conflict with Hitler and allowed him to break the Versailles settlement in 1935 and 1936. Give some indication of why you think this was. Was this sensible and understandable? The rest of the essay will add flesh to the bare bones. Once you have suggested your line of attack, the question is probably best done chronologically.

- What was Britain's attitude to Germany from 1919 to 1933 (pages 47–52)? Why was this?
- Did Hitler's coming to power in Germany make any difference to British policy? Should it have made any difference (pages 72–3)?
- How did Britain respond to Hitler's actions in 1933–4? How threatening were Hitler's actions in this period (pages 75–6)?
- Why did Britain not take a stronger line against Hitler when he announced he was rearming in 1935 (pages 77–8)?
- To what extent was Britain dependent on others, not least France, in order to make any different course of action possible (page 87)?
- What other problems did Britain face in 1935–6 (pages 79–85)?
- Why did Britain not take action when Hitler marched into the Rhineland in 1936 (pages 86–8)?

Your conclusion should pull things together. Note that the question does not specifically ask you to praise or criticise British responses, but you will lose no marks by passing comments and showing that you are aware of some of the main debates about British policy.

In the style of OCR

Study the following four passages A, B, C and D, about British attitudes towards Germany in the mid-1930s and answer the questions that follow.

Passage A

From: Sir John Simon, the Foreign Secretary, who visited Berlin in March 1935, a few weeks after Hitler's announcement of German plans for rearmament. Simon explains the major aims of British policy towards Hitler.

The object of British policy was to preserve general peace by helping to secure co-operation amongst all European countries. His Majesty's Government most earnestly wished that Germany should work with all countries for that object. They felt the future of Europe would take one of two forms ... It would either take the form of co-operation for securing continued peace – and this was the form His Majesty's Government earnestly desired. Or it would take the form of a division into camps – isolation, on the one side, and combination (which may look like encirclement) on the other.

Passage B

From: A.J.P. Taylor, English History 1914–1945, *first published in 1965. Taylor had little sympathy with British statesmen in the inter-war period.*

In April [1935] MacDonald, still just on his feet, met Mussolini and Laval, the French prime minister, and the three set up the 'Stresa front' against breaches of the international order. The meeting was a last echo of the great international gatherings with which Lloyd George had once dazzled Europe, and an odd meeting at that – three renegade Socialists defending the results of 'the war to end war and to make the world safe for democracy', two of whom had opposed the war, while the third had destroyed democracy in his own country. The 'Stresa front' was a front in the sense of a 'bold front' to conceal inner quaverings, not in the sense of 'front line', as Hitler correctly assumed. The National Government soon added their own proof. In June they concluded a private deal with Germany, limiting the German navy to 35 per cent of the British, with submarines at 45 per cent or even 100 per cent in case of danger from Russia. This, though defended as better than nothing, was an open repudiation of disarmament by international agreement and of the treaty of Versailles.

Passage C

From: Richard Overy with Andrew Wheatcroft, The Road to War, *first published in 1989. Overy and Wheatcroft try to provide a balanced view of British policy towards Germany pre-1936.*

It was evident that Germany wanted major revision of the Treaty of Versailles. Whether this extended beyond rearmament and an adjustment of the eastern frontiers to demands for the return of German colonies was less clear. In March 1935 Sir John Simon and Anthony Eden visited Hitler, who urged them to consider making colonial concessions in Africa. Simon privately suggested giving Germany Liberia. In the same visit Hitler raised the prospect of an agreement on naval armaments, first raised by the German Commander-in-Chief of the navy the previous November. Since British intelligence were in some ignorance of German naval plans the offer of a fixed ratio of 35:100 in Britain's favour was too good to resist. Hitler sent Ribbentrop to negotiate the agreement, which was finally signed in June, despite what the British saw as an unfortunate arrogance and inflexibility in the German envoy. Economic agreements extending substantial credit to Germany existed from 1933; vital raw materials and food flowed from the Empire via London to German destinations. In return Britain bought advanced German machinery. Until 1937 Hitler's strategy still incorporated the possibility of agreement with Britain, and relations between the two states were better than German relations with any other Western government. But until 1936 Hitler did not ask for anything that the British were not, in the end, willing to concede.

Passage D

From: Winston Churchill, The Gathering Storm, *first published in 1948. Churchill was critical of a host of British actions and policies with regard to Germany in the mid-1930s.*

By the Treaty of Versailles the Germans were not entitled to build more than six armoured ships of 10,000 tons, in addition to six light cruisers not exceeding 6,000 tons. The British Admiralty had recently found out that the last two pocket-battleships being constructed, the *Scharnhorst* and the *Gneisenau*, were of a far larger size than the Treaty allowed, and of a quite different type. In fact, they turned out to be 26,000-ton light battle-cruisers, or commerce-destroyers of the highest class.

   In the face of this brazen and fraudulent violation of the Peace Treaty, carefully planned and begun at least two years earlier (1933), the Admiralty actually thought it was worthwhile making an Anglo-German Naval Agreement. His Majesty's Government did this without consulting their French ally or informing the League of Nations. At the very time when they themselves were appealing to the League and enlisting the support of its members to protest against Hitler's violation of the military clauses of the Treaty they proceeded by a private agreement to sweep away the naval clauses of the same Treaty …

   The limitation of the German Fleet to a third of the British allowed Germany a programme of new construction which would set her yards to work at maximum activity for at least ten years. There was therefore no practical limitation or restraint of any kind imposed upon German naval expansion. They could build as fast as was physically possible.

1. Using these four passages and your own knowledge, assess the view that British policy towards Germany in the period 1933–6 was always unrealistic. (30 marks)
2. Assess the reasons why, in the period 1933 to 1936, British critics of appeasement had such a limited impact on British policy towards Germany. (45 marks)

Exam tips

The cross-references are intended to take you straight to the material that will help you to answer the questions.

1. Remember two things:
   - Good answers will not deal with the issues per passage but will arrange them thematically (for example, A and C agree that … whereas B and D think …).
   - You must use your knowledge of the topic to help explain and evaluate the interpretations in the passages.

   Start by making clear what you think British policy towards Germany in the period was. Source A, written by the British Foreign Secretary, provides information about British aims. Sir John Simon suggests that the main objective was to preserve peace by securing co-operation with all European countries, including Germany. Was this realistic? Aims and actions are not always the same thing. What actions did Britain take against Germany? The sources tend to focus on 1935. However, you will need to say something about British policy to Hitler pre-1935 (pages 75–6). You will then need to consider British reaction to German rearmament in 1935, incorporating the sources into your answer. Sources B and D are critical of British actions in 1935. Why? Are the criticisms fair? Source C suggests that Britain and Germany were on reasonably good terms in 1935–6. Was this the case? If so, was this sensible action? You will also have to mention Hitler's march into the Rhineland in 1936 (pages 86–7). Should Britain have taken action against him at this stage? Why was no action taken (pages 87–8)?

2. It is worth establishing at the start that you understand the question. Who were the main critics of appeasement? (It is worth naming Winston Churchill.) What action did Churchill and (a few) others want to take? Then outline the reasons why government ministers adopted a 'soft' rather than a 'hard' line to Germany. You will then need to have at least one paragraph on each of the following issues:
   - Why did Hitler not seem much of a threat in 1933 (pages 72–3)? Why were many British politicians reasonably sympathetic to Germany (page 27)?
   - What major problems, besides Germany, did Britain face in the period 1933–6 (pages 79–85)?
   - Why was Britain so dependent on others, not least France (page 87)?
   - What actions did Hitler take in the period 1933–5 and what was the British response (pages 75–8)?
   - What action did Hitler take in 1936 and what was Britain's response (pages 86–7)?
   - With the benefit of hindsight, what actions might Britain have taken against Hitler (pages 86–8)?

   Reach a conclusion. In your view, what were the main reasons why British governments acted as they did? Were these actions rational and understandable, given what was known at the time? Remember that evidence should be used in essay answers to evaluate the historical debate.

5 Chamberlain and Appeasement 1937–8

POINTS TO CONSIDER

Few issues in British foreign policy in the twentieth century are more controversial than appeasement and few Prime Ministers have been more vilified than Neville Chamberlain. This chapter will examine the policy of appeasement and the role of Neville Chamberlain in the years 1937–8. It will do so by focusing on the following themes:

- Chamberlain's aims in foreign policy
- Chamberlain's concerns in 1937–8
- The *Anschluss*
- The problem of Czechoslovakia
- The Munich conference

Key dates

1937	May	Chamberlain became Prime Minister
	July	Start of Chinese–Japanese war
1938	February	Eden resigned as Foreign Secretary; replaced by Lord Halifax
	March	Hitler annexed Austria
	Aug.–Sept.	Runciman mission to Czechoslovakia
	15 Sept.	Chamberlain met Hitler at Berchtesgaden
	22–23 Sept.	Chamberlain met Hitler at Bad Godesberg
	29–30 Sept.	Munich Conference

1 | Chamberlain's Aims in Foreign Policy

In May 1937 Stanley Baldwin retired. Neville Chamberlain succeeded him as Prime Minister. Chamberlain's family was steeped in politics. His father, Joseph Chamberlain, had been a leading late Victorian and Edwardian politician. His half-brother, Austen, had been Foreign Secretary in the 1920s. Neville had come to political life late, becoming an MP in 1918 when he was nearly 50. He had made his name first as a social reformer and then as a competent Chancellor of the Exchequer who had helped to steer Britain through the Great Depression and along the road to economic recovery.

Key question
What were Chamberlain's aims in foreign policy?

Key date
Neville Chamberlain became Prime Minister: May 1937

Chamberlain was the obvious choice for Prime Minister. He had considerable experience in high office and was widely respected within the Conservative Party and in parliament. He was seen as practical and 'safe'. He was, perhaps, a difficult man to like: serious, aloof and imperious. But he was an easy man to respect: tough, efficient and conscientious. Even Winston Churchill was lavish in his praise when seconding his nomination for the Conservative Party leadership.

Few thought that the change of Prime Minister would mean dramatic changes of policy. Chamberlain belonged to the same party as Baldwin and the two men had co-operated closely on domestic and foreign issues. Both were patriots who were wedded to the idea of the British Empire. Both hated socialism. Baldwin supported, and in many ways had groomed, Chamberlain as his successor. Chamberlain reshuffled the Cabinet but his team was essentially the same as Baldwin's. Eden remained as Foreign Secretary.

However, there were to be differences. Baldwin had lacked dynamism and, after 1935, could be accused of allowing policy to drift. Chamberlain, though 68 years old (only two years younger than Baldwin), was determined to play a more vigorous and positive role. His style contrasted sharply with that of Baldwin. He was less concerned with consensus. He was also determined to control foreign policy and not be controlled by civil servants or by his Foreign Secretary. Although he took advice from an 'inner cabinet' of ministers and friends, many saw his leadership style as autocratic. His feeble appearance belied his confidence and strength of purpose.

Chamberlain's aims

Chamberlain was not an ignorant muddler in foreign affairs as some historians have suggested. Intelligent and clear-sighted, he had been closely involved in all matters of government throughout the 1930s and, as Chancellor of the Exchequer, had been particularly good at noting the interconnections between foreign and financial policy.

It was evident to Chamberlain, as to everybody else, that soon there would be enormous changes in the relative international standing of the great powers, especially Germany. He hoped that these changes could occur without war: he loathed the prospect of war which, in his view, 'wins nothing, cures nothing, ends nothing'. Although British military intelligence exaggerated German military power, and particularly the damage the *Luftwaffe* might do to Britain, there was no doubt that Nazi Germany would be a difficult enemy to defeat in the event of war. Consequently Chamberlain was prepared to go to great lengths to preserve peace.

He was not a pacifist. If Britain's vital interests were at stake he was prepared to fight. But he hoped he could ensure, by reason and concession, that Britain's national security was not endangered. Convinced that the maintenance of peace could not be achieved without British participation in foreign affairs, he

Key term

Luftwaffe
The German air force.

Profile: Neville Chamberlain 1869–1940

1869	–	Born: half-brother of Austen Chamberlain (Foreign Secretary 1924–9)
1915	–	Became Lord Mayor of Birmingham
1917	–	Appointed Director of National Service
1918	–	Elected Conservative MP for Birmingham Ladywood constituency
1922	–	Became Postmaster General
1923	–	Served as Paymaster General and then Minister of Health
1923–4	–	Served as Chancellor of the Exchequer
1924–9	–	Served as Minister of Health
1931–7	–	Served as Chancellor of the Exchequer in the National Government
1932	–	Introduced tariff reform
1937	–	Became Prime Minister
1938	–	Attended the Munich conference
1939	–	Declared war on Germany
1940	May –	Replaced as Prime Minister by Winston Churchill
	Nov. –	Died of cancer

The word now indissolubly linked to Chamberlain's name is **'appeasement'**. For many years after the Second World War appeasement had a bad press. Those who had supported it were seen as the 'guilty men' whose misguided policies had helped to bring about war. The appeasers were portrayed as cynical defenders of the capitalist system who hoped to drive Germany and Russia into mutual destruction, or as timid cowards. Chamberlain was usually seen as guilty man number one.

However, many historians now view appeasement and Neville Chamberlain in a different and far more positive light. They point out that the main ideas of appeasement were not something that Chamberlain invented. For hundreds of years it has been a cardinal principle of British foreign policy that it is better to resolve international disputes through negotiation and compromise than through war. Some historians think that in the circumstances of 1937–8 Chamberlain had little alternative but to appease. Appeasement had its dangers, but so did all other possible courses of action. Even now it is difficult to see what realistic alternatives there were to appeasement – except war.

Key term

Appeasement A policy of giving way to hostile demands to avoid war. Primarily associated with British and increasingly also with French foreign policy in the 1930s.

determined to play a key conciliatory – or appeasing – role. He had no illusions about how difficult a task he faced, but he believed that a just settlement of many of the reasonable grievances of Germany, Italy and Japan was possible.

Chamberlain has been criticised for lacking an insight into the minds of the dictators. In his defence, Chamberlain certainly did not trust Hitler, Mussolini or the Japanese. (He soon believed Germany to be the 'bully of Europe' and Hitler 'utterly untrustworthy and dishonest'.) For this reason he was not simply intent on appeasing the dictators. He also favoured rearmament. He was convinced that 'you should never menace unless you are in a position to carry out your threat'. Until Britain was adequately armed, Chamberlain said, 'we must adjust our foreign policy to our circumstances and even bear with patience and good humour actions which we would like to treat in a very different fashion'.

Chamberlain wrote in 1937, 'I believe the double policy of rearmament and better relations with Germany and Italy will carry us safely through the dangerous period, if only the Foreign Office will play up'. He was suspicious of the Foreign Office and claimed in private that it had 'no imagination and no courage'. He was quite prepared to use his own intermediaries and communicated directly, rather than through the Foreign Office, with some ambassadors, such as Sir Nevile Henderson in Berlin. Henderson pictured Hitler as a moderate with limited aims, a man with whom it was possible to do business. Henderson's despatches probably helped to confirm Chamberlain in his policies.

Support for Chamberlain

Although Chamberlain's personal diplomacy sometimes angered the Foreign Office, there seems little doubt that the policy he pursued was supported by the great majority of the Cabinet, MPs and the British public. Recent research has suggested that the government actively manipulated public opinion through a variety of propaganda techniques in order to sustain support for appeasement policies. However, this is far from proven. What is certain is that the vast majority of the British people were repelled by the prospect of war.

Opposition to Chamberlain

Winston Churchill was the most prominent anti-appeaser. He was later to acquire the reputation of having been right on Hitler, whereas Chamberlain had been wrong. Churchill's views, however, derived more from his own preconceptions and anti-German prejudices than from a prolonged study of Hitler. There were not many in Britain who cared to go along with Churchill's hunches and prejudices in 1937–8. He had been wrong on too many occasions in the past. He was seen by many as a right-wing maverick and war-monger. Only a small, unco-ordinated cluster of Conservative MPs supported his anti-appeasement line.

The Labour Party disliked Chamberlain and hated Hitler, Mussolini and fascism. Some Labour MPs objected to Chamberlain's policy to the dictators simply because it was Chamberlain's policy. In reality, Labour proposed no real alternative, never mind consistent, course of action. Most Labour MPs opposed every initiative for increased defence spending. They preached a strong policy supported only by strong words.

The problem of allies

Chamberlain knew he could count on little support from Britain's potential allies.

Key question
Why was Chamberlain unable to find allies?

The League of Nations

Chamberlain had no confidence in the League of Nations or in collective security. When **President Roosevelt** suggested a conference to discuss world problems, Chamberlain considered the idea to be 'drivel'. He had been a businessman and liked the idea of face-to-face, business-like discussions between statesmen. The interested parties would then devise new contracts that they would thereafter make every effort to observe.

France

Throughout the 1930s France was ruled by a series of weak and short-lived governments and Chamberlain had no confidence in the country or its statesmen.

The USSR

Chamberlain had even less confidence in the USSR. He feared and distrusted Stalin and communism as much as he feared and distrusted Hitler and Nazism).

President Roosevelt
Franklin Delano Roosevelt had been elected president in 1932 and was re-elected in 1936. The USA had been badly hit by the Depression. Roosevelt's main priority in the 1930s was to get Americans back to work.

Key term

The USA

Chamberlain hoped for more from the USA. He was aware that, without US assistance in the First World War, Britain and France might well have been defeated. But he was also aware that there was little prospect of US involvement in European or world affairs. In the 1930s the USA was overwhelmingly isolationist and had no wish for foreign entanglements. Most Americans believed they had been forced into entering the First World War by big bankers and manufacturers intent on making huge profits. In the late 1930s the US Congress passed a series of Neutrality Acts preventing the USA from selling arms or giving loans to any country involved in war. These were designed to keep the USA out of any future wars.

President Roosevelt had some sympathy with Britain and France. In October 1937 he made his so-called 'quarantine' speech, calling for a concerted effort to oppose those countries who were creating 'a state of international anarchy'. However, such talk was not followed by action. Roosevelt, with a shrewd eye on US public opinion, held aloof from international commitments that might entangle the USA in foreign wars. The USA would not even join in a stand against Japanese aggression when US commercial and strategic interests were plainly threatened.

'It is always best and safest', thought Chamberlain, 'to count on nothing from the Americans but words'. However, aware of the importance of USA economic help to Britain in the First World War, he was reluctant to become involved in another European conflict without some assurances of US support.

The Dominions

In addition, Chamberlain was aware that Britain could not necessarily rely on the British Dominions, whose support had also been so important in the First World War. Canada and South Africa were reluctant to become involved in European problems, while Australia and New Zealand were more concerned with the threat from Japan than the threat from Germany.

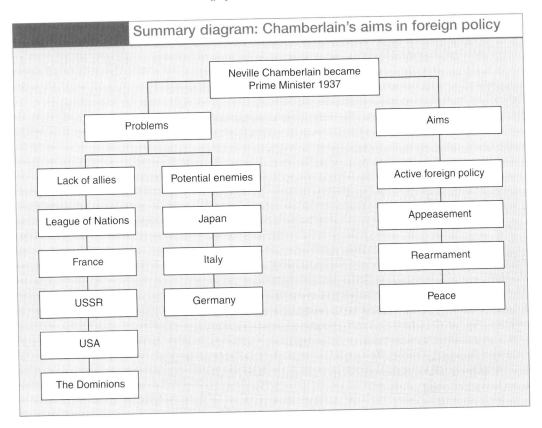

Summary diagram: Chamberlain's aims in foreign policy

2 | Chamberlain's Concerns in 1937–8

The problem of Japan

Key question
Why was Japan a problem for Chamberlain?

Key date
Start of Chinese-Japanese war: July 1937

Chamberlain immediately faced problems in the Far East. In July 1937 Chinese–Japanese hostility escalated into full-scale war, destroying any possibility of Japan being reintegrated into the international community. Japanese forces quickly took over large areas of China and Japan proclaimed her intention of securing a **new order** in East Asia.

Chamberlain seemed to have little alternative but appeasement. He was faced with a worsening situation in Europe and could not risk a conflict with Japan. His government urged restraint and appealed for an end to the conflict, but in vain. Efforts to co-ordinate policy with the USA had only limited success. The USA showed no signs of wanting to play a decisive role in East Asia. In the circumstances the best British hope was that Japan would get bogged down in a war of attrition in China, which indeed was what happened.

Key term
New order
Japan's aim for Asia, ending European imperialism, halting communism and uniting Asians in an alliance free of Western taint.

In the late 1930s British attention was focused more on Europe than on the Far East. However, Chamberlain could not avoid the fact that European and Far Eastern problems often interacted: policy in each area was influenced by the other. Fear of Japanese aggression was an important factor in understanding why Britain was keen to conciliate Italy and Germany. The awareness that many Japanese leaders felt more at home with Nazi Germany and Fascist Italy than with Britain and the other Western democracies was a further reason for caution.

Chamberlain and Hitler

Key question
How successful was Chamberlain in 1937 and early 1938?

In July 1937 Chamberlain explained to the Cabinet the impossibility of fighting Germany, Italy and Japan at the same time. The only solution was to find a way of separating these powers by diplomatic means. He intended to explore the prospects of a settlement with each potential enemy in turn. His hope was to detach them from the aggressive bloc one by one by active examination of their grievances.

In the autumn of 1937 Chamberlain sent his friend Lord Halifax, an ex-**Viceroy of India**, to visit Hitler to find out precisely what Hitler wanted. (Foreign Secretary Eden was not altogether happy about the visit by a colleague who had no responsibility for foreign affairs.) Conversations between Halifax and the Nazis ranged widely. Halifax made it clear that Britain was prepared to accept some changes in Austria, Czechoslovakia and Poland, provided the changes came about through peaceful means. Britain was also ready to consider giving Germany some colonies in Africa. (This was to be at the expense of Belgium and Portugal, rather than Britain or its Dominions.)

Viceroy of India
The governor of India, acting in the name of the sovereign.

Key term

Hitler had little interest in African colonies, but indicated that he still hoped for an agreement with Britain. He certainly seemed to pose no immediate threat. Indeed Germany had better relations with Britain than with any other Western government. The two states were important trading partners and Britain continued to provide Germany with considerable economic assistance, including credit and vital raw materials.

Chamberlain and Mussolini

Anthony Eden resigned as Foreign Secretary; replaced by Lord Halifax: February 1938

Key date

In 1937 Chamberlain spent a great deal of time trying to improve relations with Italy. Intent on (what he called) a 'new impetus', he by-passed Eden and the Foreign Office and sent a personal letter to Mussolini urging that Britain and Italy should make a serious effort to resolve their differences. Mussolini responded favourably, but the continuation of the Spanish Civil War made an Anglo-Italian accommodation difficult. In August 1937 a torpedo, believed to have been fired by an Italian submarine, narrowly missed a British destroyer off Spain. A major incident was only just averted. In January 1938 Chamberlain finally initiated Anglo-Italian talks, but the outcome was inconclusive. Mussolini wanted Italian domination of the Mediterranean and North Africa, which Britain was not prepared to concede.

Chamberlain's efforts to reach an agreement with Mussolini led to major discord with Anthony Eden who felt that his authority as Foreign Secretary was being undermined by Chamberlain's unwarranted intervention. He was also critical of Chamberlain's conduct of policy. He thought the Prime Minister should have made more effort to reach agreement with the USA and he was critical of Chamberlain's attempts to appease Mussolini. In Eden's view, the Italian leader was 'the complete gangster whose pledged word means nothing'. In February 1938 Eden resigned. In a statement to the Commons, he said 'I do not believe that we can make progress in European appeasement … if we allow the impression to gain currency abroad that we yield to constant pressure'.

Chamberlain appointed Lord Halifax in Eden's place. He also replaced the anti-German Sir Robert Vansittart with a permanent **Under-Secretary of State** of his own choosing – Sir Alec Cadogan. Chamberlain was now much more in control of foreign affairs with compliant personnel to assist him.

In April 1938 Britain and Italy finally reached agreement. Britain would recognise Italy's position in Abyssinia in return for Italy's withdrawing troops from Spain. The agreement was not to come into force until the Spanish Civil War had ended. Anglo-Italian relations improved somewhat. Nevertheless, Italy remained a potentially hostile power and Mussolini continued his military build-up in the Mediterranean. However, by the spring of 1938 German actions in central Europe had assumed a far greater significance than Italian actions in the Mediterranean.

Key term

Under-Secretary of State
A top civil servant with considerable responsibility for foreign affairs.

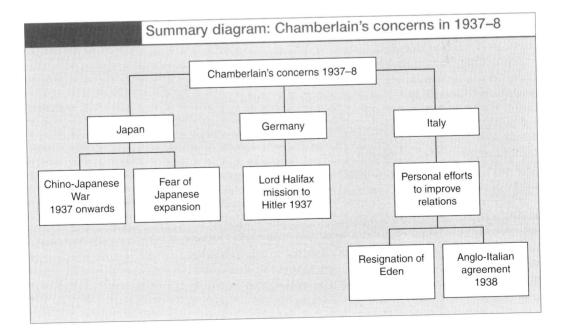

Summary diagram: Chamberlain's concerns in 1937–8

3 | The *Anschluss*

The *Anschluss* of Germany and Austria had been specifically forbidden by the Treaty of Versailles (see page 23). However, Hitler had long harboured ambitions to annex his homeland. He was encouraged by the fact that many Austrians also favoured union with Germany and that the Austrian Nazi Party had considerable support. Since 1934 the Austrian government had struggled to keep Austrian Nazis under control and German influence at bay. Until 1936 it had the support of Italy, but, as Hitler and Mussolini drew closer together, it became obvious that Austria could no longer rely on Italian help.

Throughout 1937 the Austrian Nazis, aided by money and advice from Berlin, increased their influence. By 1938 Schuschnigg, the Austrian Chancellor, felt he was losing control of the situation. In February 1938 he visited Hitler's home at Berchtesgaden in Bavaria, hoping to persuade him to restrain the Austrian Nazis. The meeting was a mistake. Hitler threatened and bullied the Austrian leader and insisted he should include Nazis in his Cabinet. Schuschnigg, shocked by Hitler's aggressive tactics, agreed to his demands and Seyss-Inquart, the Austrian Nazi leader, became Minister of the Interior.

Hitler acts: March 1938

It seems that Hitler planned to do little more at this stage. However, Schuschnigg again precipitated events. On his return to Austria, he announced that he intended to hold a plebiscite (on 13 March) to enable the Austrian people to decide whether they wished to become a part of Germany. Hitler, fearing the vote might go against him, was outraged. He demanded the cancellation of the plebiscite, whipped up opposition amongst the Austrian Nazis and threatened war.

Schuschnigg, aware that he could expect little support from Italy, Britain or France, resigned. His successor, Seyss-Inquart, immediately invited Hitler to send troops into Austria to preserve order. On 12 March, the hastily assembled German forces crossed the frontier and were enthusiastically welcomed by the Austrians. Hitler, following close behind his troops, returned in triumph to his homeland and declared the *Anschluss* of Austria and Germany. The *Anschluss*, approved by a massive majority in a plebiscite run by the Nazis, was clearly a great success for Hitler.

Reaction to the *Anschluss*

The British government had little warning of the crisis – not surprisingly, because Hitler had decided to act only at the last minute. Chamberlain was not opposed to the *Anschluss* as such, but to the way it had happened. He recognised that 'Nothing could have arrested this action by Germany unless we and others with us had been prepared to use force to prevent it'. Britain was not prepared to use the limited force she possessed. France, with a large army but without a government throughout the Austrian crisis, did nothing but protest. Mussolini, who had protected Austria in 1934, did nothing at all.

Key question
What was Britain's reaction to the *Anschluss*?

Key date

Hitler annexed Austria: March 1938

Key term

Anschluss
The union of Austria and Germany.

It was, in fact, hard to argue that a great crime had occurred when so many Austrians expressed their joy at joining the **Third Reich**. Perhaps the most important feature of the *Anschluss* was not that it had happened, but how it had happened. If one frontier could be changed in this way, why not others? Hitler's justification for the *Anschluss* was that there were large numbers of people of German stock in Austria demanding union with Germany. The uncomfortable fact was that there were similar populations of German-speaking people in other countries: Poland, Lithuania, Switzerland and, above all, Czechoslovakia.

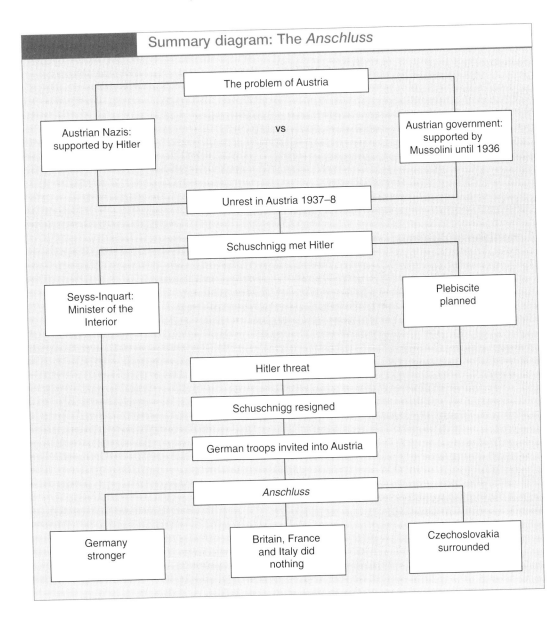

Summary diagram: The *Anschluss*

4 | The Problem of Czechoslovakia

The *Anschluss* immediately focused international attention on Czechoslovakia, much of which was now surrounded by German territory. The creation of Czechoslovakia had been, in Winston Churchill's view in 1919, 'an affront to self-determination'. By the 1930s only about half of the 15 million population of Czechoslovakia were Czechs. The country contained over two million Slovaks, 750,000 Hungarians, 500,000 Ruthenians and 100,000 Poles.

However, the largest minority ethnic group within Czechoslovakia comprised some 3.25 million Germans. Most of these occupied the Sudetenland, which had been part of Austria–Hungary until 1918. By 1938 many Sudeten Germans, claiming they were victimised by the Czechs, were demanding either greater 'home rule' or, preferably, union with Germany. They received encouragement and support from Germany, where the Nazi press launched increasingly bitter attacks on the Czech government.

President Beneš, the Czechoslovakian head of state, opposed the Sudeten German demands. He realised that if all the various ethnic groups within the country were given independence or self-rule, there would be no viable Czech state left. He was therefore determined to stand firm against German pressure.

Key question
Why was Czechoslovakia a major problem in 1938?

Chamberlain's views

Most British politicians had some sympathy with Czechoslovakia. Despite its astonishing ethnic composition and the fact that it did not treat its ethnic minorities particularly well, Czechoslovakia had preserved a democratic constitution more successfully than most other European states. It could also claim that it treated its minorities a good deal better than did most of its neighbours.

A few politicians, such as Churchill, thought Czechoslovakia worth fighting for. Chamberlain was not among that number. He had little confidence in Czechoslovakia, which he regarded as a 'highly artificial' creation, and had some sympathy for the Sudeten Germans. He was quite willing to see the Sudetenland handed over to Germany, provided this could be done by negotiation rather than by force.

In March 1938 Chamberlain told the Commons that British vital interests were not involved in Czechoslovakia. Britain had no treaty obligation to defend the Czech state and was in no position to offer serious military aid. In late March 1938 he wrote:

> You have only to look at the map to see that nothing France or we could do could possibly save Czechoslovakia from being overrun by the Germans if they want to do it ... I have therefore abandoned any idea of giving guarantees to Czechoslovakia or the French in connection with her obligations to that country.

The Chiefs of Staff agreed. On 28 March 1938 they reported to the Cabinet that:

Key term

Bohemia
A major province of
Czechoslovakia.

> We conclude that no pressure that we and our possible allies can bring to bear, either by sea, on land or in the air, could prevent Germany from invading and overrunning **Bohemia** and from inflicting a decisive defeat on the Czechoslovakian army. We should then be faced with the necessity of undertaking a war against Germany for the purpose of restoring Czechoslovakia's lost integrity and this object would only be achieved by the defeat of Germany and as the outcome of a prolonged struggle. In the world situation today it seems to us … Italy and Japan would seize the opportunity to further their own ends and that in consequence the problem we have to envisage is not that of a limited European war only, but of a World War.

Even more pessimistically, the Chiefs of Staff expressed the view that:

> Without overlooking the assistance we should hope to obtain from France and possibly other allies, we cannot foresee the times when our defence forces will be strong enough to safeguard our territory, trade and vital interests against Germany, Italy and Japan simultaneously.

France and Czechoslovakia

Chamberlain's main concern was not so much Czechoslovakia but France. The French, unlike Britain, did have an alliance with the Czechs. Chamberlain feared that if Germany invaded Czechoslovakia, France might go to its aid. Britain might then be forced to help France. A German defeat of France would tilt the European balance so overwhelmingly against Britain that it could not be contemplated. Unbeknown to Chamberlain, the French had no wish to be drawn into war over Czechoslovakia. Their strategic view was similar to the British. Czechoslovakia could not be defended. Daladier, the new French Premier, and Bonnet, his Foreign Minister, were frantically looking for ways to avoid having to honour France's obligations to Czechoslovakia. They would be delighted if Britain gave them an excuse.

Mutual mistrust made a joint stance by both Britain and France unlikely. It was not clear to Chamberlain what France intended to do if Czech independence was threatened. On the other hand, the French were not certain that Britain would support them if it came to war. To make matters worse, it was still not clear to either Britain or France precisely what German demands were. The ironic thing is that in the early spring of 1938 Hitler seems to have had no immediate designs on Czechoslovakia.

Key question
What could
Chamberlain have
done as the
Czechoslovakian
crisis developed?

Chamberlain's policy, March–September 1938

Convinced that the Sudeten issue could no longer be ignored, Chamberlain determined to get ahead of events. In late March 1938 he formulated his policy:

> My idea at present is that we should again approach Hitler following up our Halifax–Henderson conversations and say

something like this. '... It is no use crying over spilt milk and what we have to do now is to consider how we can restore the confidence you have shattered. Everyone is thinking that you are going to repeat the Austrian coup in Czechoslovakia. I know you say you aren't, but nobody believes you. The best thing you can do is to tell us exactly what you want for your Sudeten Germans. If it is reasonable we will urge the Czechs to accept it and if they do you must give us assurances that you will let them alone in future.'

The main aim of Chamberlain's policy was to extract from the Czech government concessions that would satisfy the Sudeten Germans before Hitler used force to impose a settlement. This policy had the full support of Lord Halifax, the Cabinet and the Foreign Office.

The May crisis

The flaw in Chamberlain's policy was that the Czech government was in no mood to make concessions. In May, after what proved to be false reports of German troop movements, the Czechs mobilised some of their reserves and prepared for war. Both Britain and France, fearing a German attack on Czechoslovakia, warned Hitler against making such a move.

Hitler was outraged by the Czech mobilisation and by the fact that the Western powers seemed to have won a diplomatic victory because he had stepped back from invasion – an invasion that he was not actually then planning. This May crisis seems to have been a critical factor in persuading him towards a military confrontation with Czechoslovakia. He told his chief officers. 'It is my unalterable decision to smash Czechoslovakia by military action in the near future.'

Increased tension

As the summer wore on, tension increased. The German press stepped up its campaign against Czechoslovakia, claiming that the Sudeten Germans were being persecuted. The Czech government stood firm. Daladier and Bonnet, troubled by economic and political crises within France, were quite happy to allow Britain to undertake the major initiatives in an effort to preserve European peace. From their perspective, this meant that, whatever happened, at least Britain would commit itself to involvement in eastern Europe. It might also be a way by which France could escape from the responsibilities of its alliance with Czechoslovakia.

Chamberlain and the USSR

Chamberlain has been criticised for ignoring the possibility of talks with the USSR. The Soviet Union, like France, had an alliance with Czechoslovakia and might have been prepared to support the Western powers against Hitler. However, Chamberlain distrusted Stalin, suspecting that the Russian leader hoped that Britain and France would fight Germany, which would be very much in Russian interests. The USSR, moreover, was in

Key term

Great purges
In the late 1930s Stalin imprisoned or executed millions of people who were suspected of disloyalty. Many of the USSR's chief generals were killed.

the midst of the **great purges** and there seemed little Stalin could or would do. Military experts had assured Chamberlain that the Soviet army lacked the capacity for an offensive war.

The Runciman mission

In June 1938 Britain proposed that a neutral mediator be sent to Czechoslovakia to try to resolve the crisis. The Czech government finally agreed and in August a mission led by Lord Runciman, a veteran Liberal politician with little diplomatic experience, travelled to Czechoslovakia to meet the various parties. Unfortunately neither the Sudeten Germans nor the Czechs were prepared to compromise and Runciman's mission, which lasted until mid-September, achieved little.

Key date

The Runciman mission to Czechoslovakia: August–September 1938

The threat of war

By September Chamberlain was increasingly anxious. British intelligence reported that Germany was planning a war against Czechoslovakia in early autumn. In Britain there was suddenly an awareness that a crisis was brewing. The country was divided. Some thought that Britain should support Czechoslovakia, but many, like Chamberlain, favoured the idea of self-determination for the Sudeten Germans and thought that war must be averted at almost any cost. The Prime Minister was aware that almost all the Dominions were hostile to the idea of fighting for Czechoslovakia and realised the danger of taking a divided country and a divided empire into war. In September he wrote:

> … you should never menace unless you are in a position to carry out your threats, and although, if we were to fight, I should hope we should be able to give a good account of ourselves, we are certainly not in a position in which our military advisers would feel happy … to begin hostilities if we were not forced to do so.

Key terms

Nuremberg rally
Hitler held major annual Nazi Party meetings at Nuremberg in Germany.

Martial law
The suspension of ordinary administration and policing and the imposition of military power.

Hitler kept up the pressure. This was the only way he was likely to get the Sudetenland, as it was inconceivable that Czechoslovakia would give up a large amount of its territory without German pressure. At the **Nuremberg rally** in September, he criticised the Czech government, demanded self-determination for the Sudeten Germans and assured them they would be neither defenceless nor abandoned. Hitler's speech aroused great passion in the Sudetenland and the Czech government quickly declared **martial law**. Several Germans were killed and thousands more fled to Germany with tales of brutal repression. It seemed that war between Germany and Czechoslovakia was imminent.

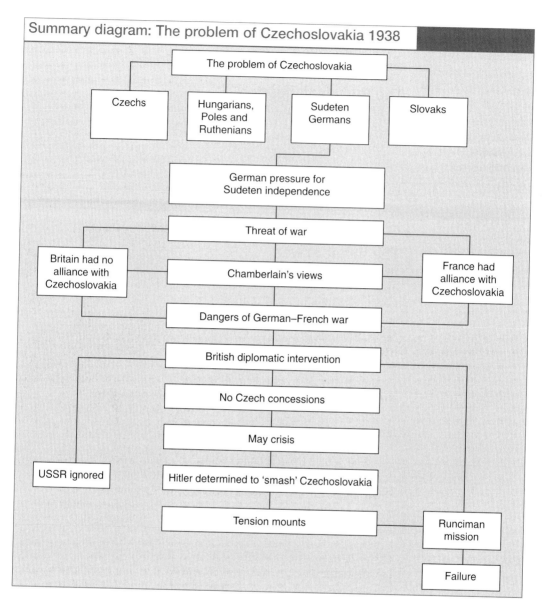

Summary diagram: The problem of Czechoslovakia 1938

The problem of Czechoslovakia

Czechs

Hungarians, Poles and Ruthenians

Sudeten Germans

Slovaks

German pressure for Sudeten independence

Threat of war

Britain had no alliance with Czechoslovakia

Chamberlain's views

France had alliance with Czechoslovakia

Dangers of German–French war

British diplomatic intervention

No Czech concessions

May crisis

USSR ignored

Hitler determined to 'smash' Czechoslovakia

Tension mounts

Runciman mission

Failure

5 | The Munich Conference

Plan Z

Chamberlain now determined to put into effect the so-called Plan Z. He would fly to Germany to meet Hitler face to face and ask him what his demands really were. This proposal, according to Chamberlain, was 'so unconventional and daring that it rather took Halifax's breath away'. In the 1930s British Prime Ministers tended to stay at home and certainly did not fly abroad. Arguably Chamberlain's plan was foolhardy: it committed Britain to imposing a negotiated settlement on the Czech government. However, Plan Z received 'unanimous and enthusiastic' approval from the Cabinet and even most Labour MPs thought it a statesman-like gesture.

Key question
Was Chamberlain right to meet Hitler to discuss the situation in Czechoslovakia?

Chamberlain met Hitler at Berchtesgaden: 15 September 1938

Key date

The 'honest broker' from London urges Czechoslovakia not to allow himself to be shot by the brutal German with the machine-gun, advising him instead to put his head into the noose marked 'capitulation'. *Izvestiya*, Moscow, 16 September 1938. How far is the Russian cartoon a fair representation of what was happening to Czechoslovakia in 1938?

Chamberlain wrote a brief note to Hitler, asking to meet him. Hitler agreed. He may have been flattered by Chamberlain's proposal; but, like Chamberlain, he may also have been uneasy at the course of events. No-one could feel even moderately certain what would happen if war broke out.

The meeting at Berchtesgaden

On 15 September 1938 Chamberlain boarded an aircraft for the first time in his life and flew to meet Hitler at Berchtesgaden. The two leaders talked for three hours and reached a rough agreement. Chamberlain accepted Hitler's main demand that all the areas in Czechoslovakia in which Germans comprised over 50 per cent of the population should be handed over to Germany. In return Hitler agreed not to attack Czechoslovakia until Chamberlain had consulted with the French and Czechs. Hitler, assuming that the Czechs would refuse to cede the Sudetenland and that Britain would then wash its hands of them, was delighted.

Chamberlain flew back to Britain and set about convincing his Cabinet, the French and finally the Czechs that Hitler's demands, if met, would produce a lasting peace. The Cabinet and the French were won over with comparative ease. The Czech government, on the other hand, was appalled at the situation. However, without French or British backing, the Czechs had little option but to accept the loss of the Sudetenland. At least Chamberlain agreed to guarantee the new (weakened) state of Czechoslovakia in the event of its being threatened in future by Germany.

The meeting at Bad Godesberg

On 22 September Chamberlain flew back to Germany to meet Hitler at Bad Godesberg on the Rhine, expecting that, 'I had only to discuss quietly with him the proposals that I had brought with me'. To Chamberlain's consternation, Hitler said the previous proposals were insufficient. (Czech concessions were not what Hitler had expected or wanted.) The claims of Poland and Hungary to Czechoslovakian territory had to be met and, in addition – to protect Sudeten Germans from Czech brutality – Hitler demanded the right to occupy the Sudetenland by force no later than 1 October.

Chamberlain met Hitler at Bad Godesberg: 22–3 September 1938

Key date

Faced with this new German ultimatum, Chamberlain returned to London. He was still in favour of accepting Hitler's demands but realised that there was now likely to be considerable opposition to such a course. This proved to be correct. Many of Chamberlain's Cabinet colleagues, angered by Hitler's bullying tactics, rejected the Godesberg proposals. Daladier also expressed doubts about the wisdom of giving in to Hitler's demands and said that France would honour its commitments to Czechoslovakia. Not surprisingly, the Czech government stated that the new proposals were totally unacceptable. War suddenly seemed likely. Both Britain and France began to mobilise. Trenches, for air-raid precautions, were dug in London parks. A few anti-aircraft guns were brought out and 38 million gas masks were distributed.

In what seemed like a last bid for peace, Chamberlain sent his personal envoy, Horace Wilson, to talk to Hitler. Wilson's mission failed. However, there was still one final hope. On 27 September the British Ambassador in Italy asked Mussolini to use his influence to persuade Hitler to reconsider. Mussolini agreed, but for a few hours it was uncertain whether his request to Hitler would have any effect. On 27 September Chamberlain broadcast to the British people:

How horrible, fantastic, incredible, it is that we should be digging trenches and trying on gas masks here because of a quarrel in a far away country between people of whom we know nothing …
I would not hesitate to pay even a third visit to Germany, if I thought it would do any good.

Key date

Munich conference: 29–30 September 1938

Key term

Four-Power Conference The conference was to involve Britain, France, Germany and Italy.

The meeting at Munich

The day after his radio bradcast, Chamberlain got his opportunity. He was speaking in the House of Commons when news came through that Hitler had accepted Mussolini's suggestion of a **Four-Power Conference** to be held at Munich to work out an agreement to the Sudeten question. The Commons erupted. Speeches of congratulation came from every side: everyone wanted to shake Chamberlain's hand. Attlee, the Labour leader, and Sinclair, the Liberal leader, blessed Chamberlain's mission. The prospect of an immediate war seemed to have been averted and it looked as though Hitler had backed down. Only Gallagher, the single Communist MP, spoke against Chamberlain going to the Munich conference.

On 29 September Chamberlain, Daladier, Hitler and Mussolini met at Munich to discuss the fate of Czechoslovakia. Beneš, the Czech leader, was not invited to the conference. Nor was Stalin. The 12 hours of talks were remarkably casual and unco-ordinated, but agreement was finally reached in the early hours of the 30 September.

The Munich agreement was very similar to Hitler's Godesberg proposals, although it did water down some of Germany's most extreme demands. The Sudeten Germans were given self-determination within Germany. German occupation of the Sudetenland was to be carried out in five stages, spread out over 10 days, rather than one. The precise borders of the new Czech state would be determined by a conference of the four powers. Beneš had no choice but to accept the Munich terms or fight alone. He chose to surrender.

Before returning to London, Chamberlain met Hitler personally and persuaded him to sign a joint declaration:

We regard the agreement signed last night and the Anglo-German Naval Agreement as symbolic of the desire of our two peoples never to go to war with one another again. We are resolved that the method of consultation shall be the method adopted to deal with any other questions that may concern our two countries and we are determined to continue our efforts to remove every possible source of difference, and thus to contribute to assure the peace of Europe.

6 | Key Debate

Was the Munich conference a 'total and unmitigated disaster'?

Failure?

The Munich agreement and Chamberlain's role in the whole Czechoslovakian crisis have been the subject of massive debate ever since. The Munich conference is usually viewed as a terrible failure for Britain. Many historians think that Chamberlain was outplayed by Hitler at almost every point. Britain had been humiliated and forced to sacrifice a friend to avert war.

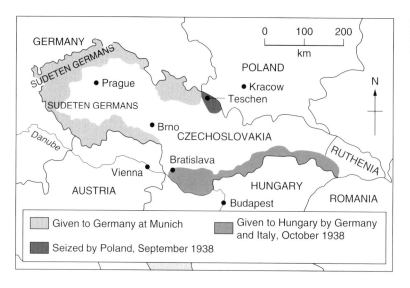

Given to Germany at Munich

Given to Hungary by Germany and Italy, October 1938

Seized by Poland, September 1938

Blessed are the peacemakers? From left to right, Chamberlain, Daladier, Hitler, Mussolini and Ciano (the Italian Foreign Minister) at the Munich conference.

Czechoslovakia had been stripped of territory, so much so that it was now indefensible. Many think that Britain should have done the honourable thing and gone to war against Germany in 1938 rather than 1939.

Success?

However, Chamberlain saw Munich as a victory rather than a defeat. Hitler had backed down and not gone to war. In the Prime Minister's view, German military superiority over Britain

'A Great Mediator'. A *Punch* cartoon, 1938. John Bull: 'I've known many Prime Ministers in my time, sir, but never one who worked so hard for security in the face of such terrible odds.' Was Chamberlain a 'great mediator'?

and France would never again be so great. He could claim that from a position of military weakness he had achieved most of his aims. He had avoided war, Germany's legitimate grievances had been settled and (most of) Czechoslovakia remained as an independent state.

In 1938 most people in Britain and France also saw Munich as a triumph rather than a defeat. Both Chamberlain and Daladier were treated as heroes on their return from the conference. Chamberlain was overcome by the large crowd that greeted him at the airport. He waved the piece of paper he had signed with Hitler and promised, 'Peace for our time'. President Roosevelt sent Chamberlain a telegram with the simple words: 'Good man'.

Chamberlain addressing the crowd at Heston, west London, after his return from Munich.

Neville Henderson, the British Ambassador in Berlin, wrote a similarly congratulatory note, but with a degree of insight: 'Millions of mothers will be blessing your name tonight for having saved their sons from the horrors of war. Oceans of ink will flow hereafter in criticism of your action.'

What would have happened if ... ?

What the likely outcome would have been of a war over Czechoslovakia in 1938 has intrigued historians ever since Munich. Many have accepted Churchill's view that it would have been better for Britain to have fought Germany in 1938 than in 1939.

- The German army was not as strong in 1938 as Chamberlain and most British military experts imagined. It was short of tanks, fuel, ammunition, trained officers and reserves.
- The *Luftwaffe* was not as strong as Britain supposed. It was not ready or able to launch a serious attack on Britain (see Table 5.1).
- Most German diplomats and generals were worried by the prospect of war.
- The French army was still the largest and best equipped in Europe.
- Czech forces were far from negligible. The Czechs had a strong defence line along the German frontier.
- Russia might have joined the war on Czechoslovakia's side.

Table 5.1: German air strength in August–September 1938

	Actual German air strength August 1938		British estimates of German air strength September 1938	
	Total	Combat ready	Total	Combat ready
Fighters	643	453	810	717
Bombers	1157	582	1235	1019
Dive-bombers	207	159	247	227

However, it is far from certain that Britain and France would have been successful in 1938.

- Neither country was ready for war.
- In 1938 Britain was virtually defenceless against air attack. It had few fighter aircraft and very little **radar** defence.
- Czech armed forces were weak and divided; most Sudeten Germans and Slovaks preferred to fight against the Czechs than for them. Czech border defences were situated in the Sudetenland and were by no means complete. The Germans anticipated over-running Czechoslovakia in little more than 10 days. French forces, deployed along the Maginot Line, could have done little to help.
- It is far from certain that Russia would have come to Czechoslovakia's assistance. Neither Poland nor Romania was prepared to tolerate Russian troops in their territory, so it would have been difficult for Russia to have sent direct help.
- Several of the British Dominions were reluctant to fight over Czechoslovakia.
- The British public was far from united in its determination to fight.

It can thus be claimed (although this was not Chamberlain's intention) that Munich bought valuable time for Britain to bolster its defences. Interestingly, Hitler did not view Munich as a great triumph. Although he had gained the Sudetenland in return for nothing save a promise of future good conduct, he had been denied a military triumph. He was confident that he could have defeated Czechoslovakia quickly and regretted his decision to reach agreement at Munich.

The aftermath of Munich

Chamberlain was not convinced that Munich made peace more secure. He seems to have had few illusions about Hitler and feared that he would not be content with his recent gains. In private he regretted using the terms 'peace with honour' and 'peace for our time' in the euphoria of his return from Germany. However, he remained confident that he, and perhaps he alone, could handle the difficult problems that undoubtedly lay ahead. At least Munich gave him a breathing space. He would continue to hope and work for peace. With the Czechoslovakian problem out of the way, it might be possible to make further progress 'along the road to sanity'.

Key term

Radar
The use of high-powered radio pulses for locating objects (for example, enemy planes).

Key question
What were the immediate results of Munich?

Opposition to Munich

Some MPs were critical of the Munich agreement. Churchill described the whole conduct of British policy as a 'total and unmitigated disaster'. Labour leaders censured Chamberlain for failing to obtain better terms, although no-one suggested what better terms might have been obtained. Many Conservatives were uneasy that Hitler's bully-boy tactics seemed to have worked. In the event, however, only Duff Cooper, First Lord of the Admiralty, resigned, and fewer than 30 Conservatives abstained rather than support the motion by which the Commons approved the policy whereby war had been averted and peace was being sought. The press was far from unanimous in support of Munich. *The Daily Worker, Reynolds News*, the *Manchester Guardian* and the *Daily Herald* were critical. Even the conservative *Daily Telegraph* had reservations. But the majority of newspapers, both national and local, supported Chamberlain's policy and actions.

British public opinion in 1938–9

It is difficult to tell how the majority of people in Britain viewed the Munich agreement. Chamberlain certainly suffered no run of by-election disasters after September 1938. There was undoubtedly great relief that war had been averted and many gave Chamberlain credit for the preservation of peace. However, most Britons seem to have distrusted Hitler and to have feared for the future. Public opinion polls, still in their infancy at this time, do seem to indicate an anti-German swing from October 1938 onwards (see Table 5.2).

Table 5.2: Opinion poll results 1938–9

Hitler says he has 'No more territorial ambitions in Europe'. Do you believe him? (October 1938)

- Yes 7%
- No 93%

In the present situation do you favour increase expenditure on armaments? (October 1938)

- Yes 72%
- No 18%
- No opinion 10%

Which of these statements comes nearest to representing your views of Mr Chamberlain's policy of appeasement? (February 1939)

1 It is a policy which will ultimately lead to enduring peace in Europe – 28%
2 It will keep us out of war until we have time to rearm – 46%
3 It is bringing war nearer by whetting the appetite of the dictators – 24%

Chamberlain's efforts to maintain peace 1938–9

In the autumn of 1938 Chamberlain's main concern was not opposition at home, but whether Hitler would abide by the terms and spirit of the Munich agreement. He continued to work for improved relations with Germany. Britain still held out the prospect of a return of some German colonies and there were Anglo-German talks on industrial, financial and trade links. The British government also welcomed and encouraged an improvement in relations between France and Germany. In December 1938 Ribbentrop, the German Foreign Minister, visited Paris and signed a Franco-German agreement expressing mutual goodwill and respect for frontiers.

Meanwhile, Chamberlain worked hard to improve relations with Italy. In November he proposed the implementation of the Anglo-Italian agreement of April 1938. While his critics questioned the extent to which the previously stated British conditions had been satisfied, his action had the overwhelming support of the House of Commons. In January 1939 Chamberlain and Lord Halifax visited Italy and met Mussolini. Mussolini welcomed them but was not impressed. 'These are the tired sons of a long line of rich men and they will lose their empire', he said. Chamberlain, by contrast, was pleased with the reception he received from the Italian crowds and thought there was a good chance of detaching Mussolini from Hitler.

In public Chamberlain and members of his government continued to talk hopefully of Hitler and Mussolini's peaceful intentions. Their aim was to avoid any increase in tension. However, the actions of Hitler in particular gave little cause for optimism. The German leader refused to make even the smallest sign of goodwill to Britain. Instead he made a number of anti-British speeches and the German press continued to make venomous attacks on Britain. Events in Germany on the night of 9–10 November 1938 further damaged Anglo-German relations. Following the killing by a Jew of a German diplomat in Paris, Jewish shops throughout Germany were wrecked and synagogues set on fire. 'Crystal Night', as the Nazi anti-Jewish **pogrom** became known, appalled most British people and destroyed any remaining goodwill for Germany in Britain.

Key term

Pogrom
An organised massacre of Jews.

Summary diagram: The Munich conference

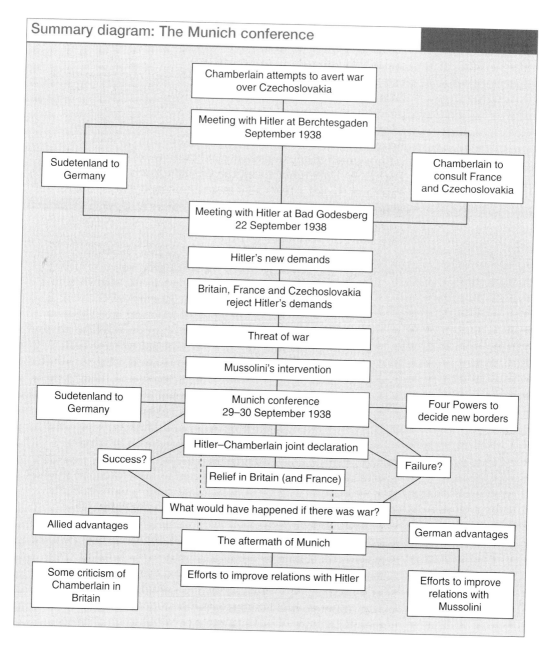

Study Guide: Advanced Level Questions

In the style of AQA

Read the following source material and then answer the questions that follow.

Source A

From: A.J.P. Taylor, The Origins of the Second World War, *published in 1969.*

The British position [on the fate of Czechoslovakia] was complicated ... morality counted for a great deal. The British statesmen used practical arguments: the danger from air attack;

the backwardness of their rearmament; the impossibility, even if adequately armed, of helping Czechoslovakia. But these arguments were used to reinforce morality, not to silence it. British policy over Czechoslovakia originated in the belief that Germany had a moral right to the Sudeten German territory, on grounds of national principle.

Source B

A cartoon by David Low published in the *Evening Standard* newspaper, July 1938. Low was critical of the Munich agreement. The figure in the cartoon represents the British public. (David Low, *Evening Standard*, 18 July 1938, Centre for the Study of Cartoons and Caricature, University of Kent.)

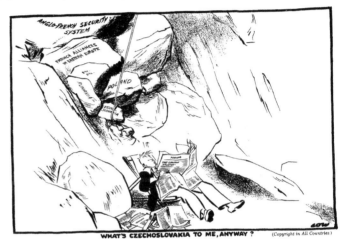

WHAT'S CZECHOSLOVAKIA TO ME, ANYWAY ?   *(Copyright in All Countries.)*

Source C

From: Anthony Adamthwaite, The Making of the Second World War, *published in 1977.*

Although the hysterical relief which greeted Munich testified to the strength of support for appeasement, this does not mean that no other policy was possible at the time. Enough attention has not been paid to the question whether, given other men in power in Britain and France, with other conceptions guiding them, the climate of opinion might not have been different. Winston Churchill's 'grand alliance' against Germany offered an alternative to appeasement. The Cabinet Foreign Policy Committee discussed the idea in the week after the *Anschluss*. No one spoke up for it and it was never thoroughly explored because it ran completely counter to the goal of *détente*.*
[*Keeping good relations with another state.]

(a) **Use Source A and your own knowledge.**
How valid is the interpretation offered by Taylor about the motives of the British government during the Sudeten crisis?   (10 marks)

(b) **Use Source B and your own knowledge.**
How useful is Source B as evidence of British public opinion about the issue of Czechoslovakia?   (10 marks)

(c) **Use Sources A, B and C and your own knowledge.**
'A cruel necessity'. Do you agree with this judgement
on the Munich agreement? (20 marks)

Exam tips

The cross-references are intended to take you straight to the material that will help you to answer the questions.

[Note: This Unit 6 AQA question is based on historiography. You should be aware of the views of different historians (particularly those mentioned in AQA's set reading material) and when asked to 'use your own knowledge' in answers you should draw on these differing views.]

1. In question **(a)** you must first explain Taylor's interpretation, then assess it with the help of your own knowledge of the views of other historians. In many respects Taylor was right. Morality was an issue for Chamberlain: he did think that Germany had a good claim to the Sudetenland. However, he also feared war and had major concerns over Britain's defences. You will need to identify the main reasons why Chamberlain supported appeasement, both before – and during – the Sudeten crisis.

2. In question **(b)** Low's cartoon was produced before the Munich agreement. Given that Low presents Czechoslovakia as the keystone of Britain's security, his cartoon should be seen as critical of the Munich agreement. There certainly were critics of Chamberlain's policies. These included members of Chamberlain's own party (like Churchill and Eden) as well as members of the Labour Party. However, most British newspapers, and thus most cartoonists, supported Chamberlain in September–October 1938. You might reflect on the extent to which cartoonists (and newspapers) seek to influence and shape public opinion, rather than simply reflect it.

3. For question **(c)** Source C suggests that there were alternatives to appeasement in 1938. It suggests that Churchill's idea of a 'grand alliance' was a feasible proposition. However, relatively few leading British or French statesmen at the time thought Churchill's idea feasible. (Source C accepts this. The idea was discussed by foreign policy experts but no one spoke up for it.) The main problem was that the USA (page 100) and the USSR (page 100) were not exactly enthusiastic proponents of the 'grand alliance' notion. Nor could the USSR be trusted (pages 108–9). Were there any other alternatives to appeasement – except war? Would it have been in Britain's best interests to have gone to war with Germany in September 1938 (pages 116–17)? Remember that you will need to refer to the views of different historians to gain the highest marks.

In the style of Edexcel

How far do you agree with the view that British policy towards Germany in the period 1931–8 underwent a major change following the appointment of Chamberlain as Prime Minister in May 1937? (60 marks)

Exam tips

The cross-references are intended to take you straight to the material that will help you to answer the question.

You will need to examine British policy in the period 1931–7. To what extent did MacDonald and Baldwin support appeasement-type policies with regard to Germany:

- before Hitler came to power in 1933 (pages 67–8)?
- after Hitler came to power and before 1937 (pages 72–91)?

Did Chamberlain adopt new policies in 1937 (pages 96–9)? You will also need to say something about the problems Chamberlain faced in 1938, namely:

- the *Anschluss* (pages 104–5)
- the Czech crisis (pages 106–13).

You might also need to consider the following issues:

- To what extent did the Austrian and Czech crises impact on British policy?
- Did Chamberlain pursue appeasement with more vigour, in the light of changed circumstances, after the *Anschluss*?

Your conclusion, which you should have indicated in your introduction, might be that there was no revolutionary change in British policy after Chamberlain came to power in 1937. However, given the growing challenge from Hitler, Chamberlain pursued a far more active role than his predecessors.

In the style of OCR

Study the following four Passages A, B, C and D, about the position and policies of Neville Chamberlain before and after the Munich Conference of October 1938, and answer the sub-questions that follow.

Passage A

From: The minutes of the Cabinet meeting held on 3 October 1938. Chamberlain here is explaining his views on rearmament.

Ever since he had become Chancellor of the Exchequer in 1931, the Prime Minister had been oppressed with the sense that the burden of armaments might break our backs. This had been one of the factors which had led him to the view that it was necessary to try and resolve the causes which were responsible for the armaments race. The Prime Minister thought that we were now in a more hopeful position and the contacts which had been established with the Dictator Powers had opened up the possibility that we might be able to reach some agreement with them which would stop the armaments race. It was clear, however, that it would be madness to stop rearming until we were convinced that other powers would act in the same way. That, however, was not the same thing as to say that we should at once embark on a great increase in our armaments programme.

Passage B

From: L.B. Namier, Diplomatic Prelude 1938–9, *published in 1948. Namier comments critically on Chamberlain and his response to the Munich agreement.*

When Chamberlain waved his 'treaty' with Hitler like a happy autograph hunter – 'Here is the paper which bears his name' – Europe was astounded. Could Chamberlain's trust, joy and triumph be genuine? His experience was that of a middle class businessman and he infused into politics the atmosphere of the 'pleasant Sunday afternoon', dull and sober. He was shrewd, ignorant and self-opinionated and had the capacity to deceive himself as much as was required by his purpose and also deceive those who chose to be deceived. Once more he secured a great and miserable victory over Churchill. But within him there was an uneasy, unclear compromise which he preferred not to probe: if he was so happy about Munich, why re-arm? If he was playing for time, why make such a poor use of it?

Passage C

From: D. Watt, How War Came, *published in 1989. Watt argues that Chamberlain's strategy towards Germany after Munich was based on a realistic view of Hitler and of Britain's diplomatic and military position at that time.*

Neville Chamberlain returned from Munich to the kind of triumph that even successful politicians can only dream of. Even he was carried away by it. The Anglo-German Agreement which he sprang on Hitler on September 30 was intended as a test. 'If he signs it and sticks to it, that will be fine', he told his private secretary. 'But if he breaks it that will convince the Americans of the kind of man he is.' In the House of Commons on October 6 he asked that remarks made in the excitement of the moment should not be taken too literally. As the enthusiasm ebbed away, Chamberlain was left with two convictions. First, that the utmost must be done to exploit the Anglo-German Agreement and to build towards a European settlement. Second, that the circumstances which forced Munich on Britain must not be left unrepaired. The first demanded the taking up of contacts with Hitler and Mussolini. The second demanded that everything possible be done to strengthen France and to accelerate the process of British rearmament. It also demanded, though it took Halifax a long time to convince Chamberlain of this, a mending of the fences with Soviet Russia.

Passage D

From: F. McDonough, Neville Chamberlain. Appeasement and the British Road to War, *published in 1998. McDonaugh argues that, after Munich, Chamberlain remained committed to the policy of appeasement.*

It is important to examine what Chamberlain expected to flow from Munich. It seems that he believed that Hitler was anxious for British friendship. It is also equally apparent that Chamberlain had not lost faith in conciliation and diplomacy as the best weapons to prevent war. On 3 October, Chamberlain believed 'contacts with the Dictator Powers had opened up the possibility that we might be able to reach some agreement with them which would stop the armaments race'. On 31 October, Chamberlain told the Cabinet: 'Our foreign policy was one of appeasement', with the central aim of 'establishing relations with Dictator Powers which will lead to a settlement in Europe'. What Chamberlain wanted, above all, was 'more support for my policy and not a strengthening of those who don't believe in it'. He was not as harassed by doubts over appeasement as many of his colleagues.

(a) Using these four passages and your own knowledge, explain why the Munich agreement has caused so much controversy. (30 marks)

Source: OCR, June 2002

(b) Assess the view that Neville Chamberlain's policy towards Germany in the years 1937 and 1938 was in Britain's best interests. (45 marks)

Exam tips
The cross-references are intended to take you straight to the material that will help you to answer the questions.

1. You must refer to the passages. Take note of just how much the introduction to each of the sources tells you about the contents.
    - Passage A provides you with details of Chamberlain's own thinking in October 1938. Is he optimistic or pessimistic – and why?
    - Passage B is critical. What are the main criticisms of Munich and Chamberlain?
    - Passage C is more positive about Chamberlain's achievements. Why?
    - Passage D suggests that Chamberlain had no intention of changing his basic policy.
    Your own knowledge is also essential. Why has the Munich agreement caused so much controversy? (Note that the Munich agreement and appeasement are almost synonymous.)
    - What are the main arguments for and against appeasement (pages 97–9)?
    - What are the main arguments for and against Chamberlain's actions at Munich (pages 113–17)?
    - What were Chamberlain's main hopes after the Munich agreement (pages 117–19)?

Now try to link your own knowledge with the information from the passages, integrating your understanding – and assessment of the value – of the passages into the body of your answer as you go along.

- Was appeasement a sensible policy? (Passage B suggests not; C is more positive.)
- Should Chamberlain be praised or blamed for the Munich agreement? (Passage B is critical: C is more positive – why? Passages A and D suggest that Chamberlain was pleased with the Munich agreement – why?)
- What did Chamberlain intend to do next? (Passage A provides Chamberlain's own thoughts in Cabinet. Passage D argues that Chamberlain intends to continue his appeasement policies. Passage C suggests that Chamberlain has some options post September 1938. Passage B remains pessimistic.)

2. Briefly outline in your introduction what Chamberlain's policy to Germany was in the years 1937 and 1938 (i.e. briefly define appeasement). Give some indication of whether you consider appeasement to be in Britain's best interests, or not. Other paragraphs should include the following issues:
- What were Chamberlain's aims? Were they sensible (pages 97–9)?
- What problems did Chamberlain face in 1937–8? To what extent did these problems affect his policy towards Germany (pages 101–4)?
- What effect did the *Anschluss* have on Chamberlain's policy? Was Chamberlain's response to the *Anschluss* sensible and understandable (pages 104–5)?
- How did Chamberlain try to deal with the Czech crisis between March and September 1938? Were his actions sensible (pages 106–13)?
- Was Munich an unmitigated disaster (pages 113–17)?

Reach a conclusion. In your view should Chamberlain be praised or blamed for his policy to Germany in the years 1937–8, and why?

Remember that evidence should be used in essay answers to evaluate the historical debate.

6 The Coming of War 1939

POINTS TO CONSIDER
This chapter should give you an understanding of the events that led Britain to declare war on Germany in September 1939. It should also enable you – finally – to assess the wisdom of appeasement and the statesmanship of Neville Chamberlain. As you read the chapter try to identify what Chamberlain could have done that was different. Should Britain have gone to war in 1939? To what extent was Chamberlain to blame for the Second World War? The chapter has been divided into the following themes:

- The uneasy peace, January–March 1939
- The end of Czechoslovakia
- The Polish guarantee
- The drift to war
- Anglo-Soviet relations
- The outbreak of war

Key dates

1939	March	The end of Czechoslovakia
		British guarantee to Poland
	April	Britain introduced conscription
	May	The Pact of Steel between Germany and Italy
	August	The Nazi–Soviet Pact
	1 Sept.	Germany invaded Poland
	3 Sept.	Britain and France declared war on Germany

Key question
Why did Hitler continue to pose a threat in early 1939?

1 | The Uneasy Peace, January–March 1939

In early 1939 Chamberlain received a number of disturbing (and incorrect) reports from British intelligence services predicting German moves against Poland, Czechoslovakia, the Ukraine, and even the Netherlands or Switzerland. In February the Cabinet agreed that a German attack on the Netherlands or Switzerland would lead to a British declaration of war. Foreign Secretary Lord Halifax, who was beginning to emerge as a political force in his own right, thought definite and clear limits should be placed on

Germany's ambitions. While his views are sometimes seen as diverging from those of Chamberlain, in reality his thinking was not very different. Neither man was prepared to give Hitler a totally free hand.

Britain and France

In the circumstances, Britain drew even closer to France. Both countries had common commitments to democracy and common fears about their own security. However, Anglo-French relations had been marked by years of mistrust. French politicians believed Britain might well leave them in the lurch and thought the British were not prepared to repeat the great 'effort of blood' made in the First World War.

Many British politicians, in return, were suspicious of the French. Chamberlain thought that France 'never can keep a secret for more than half an hour – nor a government for more than nine months'. As late as November 1938 the British Chiefs of Staff were opposed to conducting talks with France in too much detail for fear of being committed to a French war plan over which they had no control. In addition there were fears in London that France might be losing the will to resist Germany. Some French politicians seemed prepared to accept German predominance in eastern Europe. However, most were not. In 1938 pacifism had been the prevailing mood in France; but in 1939 the public mood swung in favour of resisting Nazi expansion. Most Frenchmen feared that if Germany gobbled up more territory in the east, she might ultimately prove too strong in the West.

The French government was anxious to obtain firmer pledges of British support. In particular, it wanted Britain to commit itself to sending a large army to defend France. In February Chamberlain accepted that in the event of war Britain would have to help France defend its territory. He agreed to open detailed military talks with the French. Britain also committed itself to raising an army of 32 divisions. This was a radical change in Britain's defence policy. Commitment to sending a large army to fight on the Continent, avoided for 20 years, was accepted.

British rearmament

Chamberlain, unlike many of his critics on the political left, had favoured British rearmament. After Munich he was more determined than ever that the pace of rearmament should not slacken. The best policy, he thought, was 'to hope for the best but be prepared for the worst'. In his view the main purpose of rearmament was to deter Hitler.

Much of the increase in the number of aircraft in 1938–9 came from the maturing of plans which had been made in 1935. British rearmament had long been geared to reach its peak in 1939–40. But Britain's spending on rearmament rose considerably after October 1938. The production of aircraft increased from 240 a month in 1938 to 660 a month in September 1939. By the end of 1939 British aircraft production was expected to, and indeed did,

Key question
How successful were British rearmament efforts in 1938–9?

overtake German production. This was partly because of increased emphasis on building fast fighter aircraft (Hurricanes and Spitfires) which were only a quarter of the cost of heavy bombers.

Table 6.1: Contemporary estimates of land forces 1938–9 (Divisions)

	January 1938	April 1939
Germany	81	120–130
Italy	73	85
France	100	100
Britain*	2	16
USSR	125	125
Czechoslovakia	34	–
Poland	40	40

*British forces available for the Continent.

Table 6.2: Contemporary estimates of air strengths 1935–9

Year	France	Germany	Britain	Italy	USSR
1935	1696	728	1020	1300	1700
1936	1010	650	1200	–	–
1937	1380	1233	1550	1350	–
1938	1454	3104	1606	1810	3280
1939	1792	3699	2075	1531	3361

Table 6.3: Contemporary estimates of naval strengths in 1939

	Capital ships	Aircraft carriers	Submarines
Germany	5	–	65
Italy	4	–	104
France	7	1	78
Britain	15	6	57
USSR	3	–	18
United States	15	5	87
Japan	9	5	60

Britain's radar defences improved considerably. In September 1938 only the Thames estuary had radar. By September 1939, a radar chain ran from the Orkneys to the Isle of Wight. There was suddenly the real possibility that the German bomber would not always get through. Nevertheless in November 1938, Sir John Anderson was brought into the Cabinet and put in charge of air raid precautions. Plans were made for the evacuation of children from large cities in the event of war. Gas masks were distributed, air raid shelters were dug and air raid officials were recruited and trained.

From 1936 to 1938 British intelligence had consistently exaggerated Germany's potential strength. However, after Munich it arrived at a more realistic assessment. It seemed that Germany, like Italy, faced a growing economic crisis and would not be able to risk, let alone sustain, a major war. In a long war of attrition, Britain and France's economic strength and the power of the naval blockade should ensure eventual victory.

By 1939, therefore, Chamberlain was much more confident of Britain's capacity to fight, and in particular to resist air attack. As a result, he may have been prepared to take a firmer line than in 1938. But he still hoped for, and talked of, peace. In early March 1939, he predicted that Europe was 'settling down to a period of tranquility'.

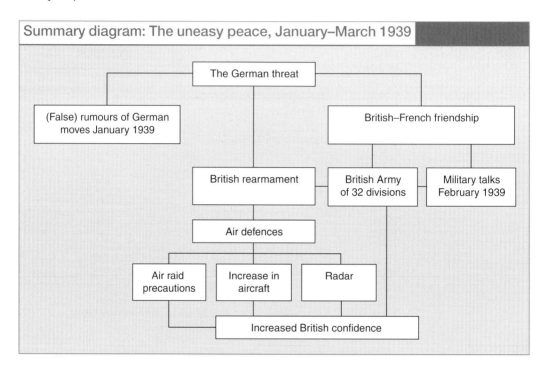

Summary diagram: The uneasy peace, January–March 1939

2 | The End of Czechoslovakia

Without its defences in the Sudetenland, Czechoslovakia was at Germany's mercy. It also faced serious internal problems. Many Slovaks had little love for what they saw as a Czech-dominated state. After Munich, Hitler deliberately encouraged the Slovaks to seek independence from Czechoslovakia. Poland and Hungary also continued to lay claim to Czechoslovakian territory. By early March the situation was so bad, internally and externally, that President Hacha, who had replaced President Beneš, proclaimed martial law. This desperate attempt to preserve the unity of Czechoslovakia actually speeded its downfall. Hitler instructed the Slovak nationalist leaders to appeal to Germany for protection and to declare independence from Czechoslovakia. At the same time Hungary issued an ultimatum demanding Ruthenia.

With his country falling apart, Hacha asked for a meeting with Hitler, hoping the German leader might do something to help Czechoslovakia. Hitler received Hacha in the small hours of 15 March. He told him that the German army intended to enter the country in a few hours' time and that his only choice was war or a peaceable occupation. Hacha broke down under the threats and

Key question
Why did the end of Czechoslovakia have such an impact on Chamberlain?

The end of Czechoslovakia: March 1939

Key date

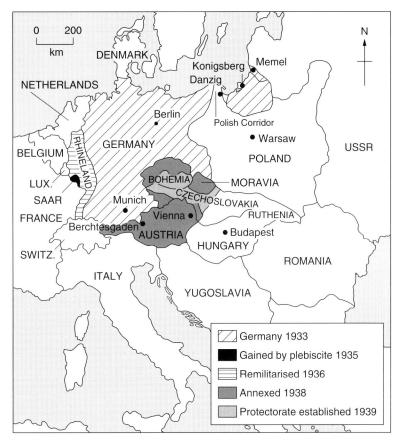

Figure 6.1: Germany 1933–9

seems to have suffered a minor heart attack. He recovered and signed a paper entrusting the fate of the Czech people to Hitler. On 15 March, German troops entered Czechoslovakia on the pretext that it was on the verge of civil war. Hitler established a German **protectorate** of Bohemia and Moravia. Slovakia was nominally independent, but under German protection. Hitler allowed Hungary to take Ruthenia.

British reaction

Hitler's take-over of Czechoslovakia had important repercussions. He had clearly ignored the Munich agreement (page 113), broken a signed agreement with Chamberlain and dismembered a small neighbour without warning or provocation. Moreover, this time he could not claim that he was uniting Germans within one German state. There was a sense of outrage in Britain as a whole and a marked shift of opinion in the Conservative Party and in the press. Most British people now felt that something must be done to stop Hitler before he controlled the whole of Europe.

Chamberlain's immediate pronouncement in the House of Commons was mild. He made it clear that there was no question of going to war. Czechoslovakia had collapsed as a result of internal disruption that freed the British government from any

---

Key term

Protectorate
A territory administered by another, usually much stronger, state. Consequently, its inhabitants are not citizens of the stronger state.

obligation. His apparent 'soft' line angered many MPs, and he faced pressure from the press, the Conservative Party, the Foreign Office and even from within his own Cabinet to do or say something stronger. All this clearly had an effect on Chamberlain. He would certainly have had political problems if he had continued meekly to accept Hitler's latest action. However, arguably he did not simply cave in to public pressure. He was indignant himself at the turn of events and Hitler's total disregard of the Munich agreement. His anger and determination to resist further German aggression was made clear at a speech he made at Birmingham on 17 March, the day before his seventieth birthday:

> Germany under her present regime has sprung a series of unpleasant surprises upon the world. The Rhineland, the Austrian *Anschluss*, the severance of the Sudetenland – all these things shocked and affronted public opinion throughout the world. Yet, however much we might take exception to the methods which were adopted in each of these cases, there was something to be said, whether on account of racial affinity or of just claims too long resisted, for the necessity of a change in the existing situation.
>
> But the events which have taken place this week in complete disregard of the principles laid down by the German government itself seem to fall into a different category, and they must cause us all to be asking ourselves: 'Is this the end of an old adventure, or is it the beginning of a new? Is this the last attack upon a small state, or is it to be followed by others? Is this in fact, a step in the direction of an attempt to dominate the world by force? It is only six weeks ago that … I pointed out that any demand to dominate the world by force was one which the democracies must resist.
>
> I feel bound to repeat that, while I am not prepared to engage this country by new unspecified commitments, yet no greater mistake could be made than to suppose that, because it believes war to be a senseless and cruel thing, this nation has so lost its fibre that it will not take part to the utmost of its power in resisting such a challenge if it ever were made.

The next day the British and French governments delivered sharp protests to Germany. Chamberlain told the Cabinet that his hopes of working with Hitler were over: 'No reliance could be placed on any of the assurances given by the Nazi leader'.

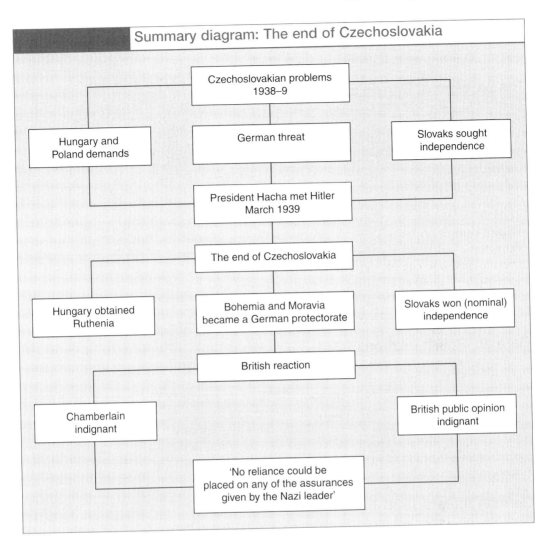

Summary diagram: The end of Czechoslovakia

3 | The Polish Guarantee

The threat to Romania?

On 17 March there was a rumour that Germany was about to deliver an ultimatum to Romania. The effects of this – totally false – rumour on the Foreign Office were electric. On 20 March Chamberlain proposed that Britain, France, Poland and Russia should issue a joint declaration that if there was a threat to the independence of any European state they would consult immediately on the steps to be taken. The British plan came to nothing. Poland had no wish to make any agreement with Russia. Stalin was also reluctant to commit himself.

Memel

In March 1939 Hitler issued an ultimatum demanding that Memel, a town given to Lithuania after 1919, should be handed back to Germany. On 21 March Lithuania returned Memel. Britain and France took no action. It was inconceivable to think of going to war over Memel, a German city to which Hitler could lay reasonable claim. However, Poland now seemed to be Hitler's next target – and this was another matter.

The problem of Danzig and the Polish Corridor

There were some 800,000 Germans in Poland. The so-called Polish Corridor divided East Prussia from the rest of Germany. Danzig was 96 per cent German, and, although nominally a Free City under the supervision of the League of Nations, had been run by the Nazis since 1934. However, Poland controlled Danzig's trade and foreign relations. This was a complicated and unsatisfactory arrangement, liable to create friction even with goodwill on all sides. No German government, whatever its political complexion, was likely to accept the Danzig solution as permanent, and Hitler's government was no exception. Polish governments were equally determined that things should remain as they were. The loss of Danzig to Germany might well compromise the rest of the gains Poland had made from Germany in 1919.

German–Polish relations 1933–8

German relations with Poland had been remarkably friendly since the signing of the German–Polish non-aggression treaty in 1934 (see page 76). On a number of occasions, Germany had suggested to the Poles that the agreement might be turned into an alliance against Russia, but the Poles did not take up these suggestions. Polish foreign policy was chiefly concerned with avoiding any commitment either to Germany or to Russia which might involve Poland in future conflict.

German threats 1938–9

After Munich, Hitler assumed that Poland would be drawn into the German orbit. In October 1938 German Foreign Minister Ribbentrop asked the Poles to give up Danzig. In return Poland would receive guarantees of its borders, German friendship and the prospect of territory in the Ukraine. In January 1939 Hitler met Colonel Beck, the Polish Foreign Minister, and added a demand for a German-controlled road or rail link across the Polish Corridor between East Prussia and the rest of Germany. To Hitler's surprise, the Poles refused to consider these relatively moderate suggestions. The Polish government was not willing for Poland to become a German **satellite**.

German demands now became more insistent and uncompromising, but as yet there were no threats. In secret Hitler admitted that he was not simply after Danzig. The whole question of living space in the east was at stake. He needed Polish economic and labour resources. He was quite prepared to compel Poland, by force if necessary, to come within the German sphere. However, at this stage he hoped for a diplomatic rather than a military triumph. He did not want or expect a general European war.

Satellite
A country that is subordinate to another.

Key term

However, tension mounted. The Polish government rejected the German proposals on Danzig and the Corridor and declared that any German attempt to alter the status of Danzig would lead to war. By the end of March there were rumours that a German attack on Poland was imminent. Britain and France feared that Poland might be overrun or forced to make terms with Germany unless they came to its support.

Key question
Was the Polish guarantee wise or foolish?

The guarantee

On 31 March Britain took the unprecedented step of offering a guarantee to Poland: if it were the victim of an unprovoked attack, Britain would come to its aid. The French government offered a similar guarantee. The Polish government, still in secret negotiations with Germany over Danzig, accepted the British and French offers.

Criticism of the Polish guarantee

The Polish guarantee was condemned by a few at the time and by many since. Of all the east European states, Poland, a right-wing military dictatorship and very **anti-Semitic**, was probably the one that Britain liked least. In fact, until 1939 Poland had few friends – except Germany.

Key terms

Anti-Semitic
Anti-Jewish.

Blank cheques
Literally a signed cheque in which the sum is not filled in. The recipient can thus fill in the amount. In diplomatic terms, it means complete freedom to act as one thinks best.

U-turn
A complete change in direction.

- Poland had distanced herself from the League of Nations.
- It had accepted Japanese and Italian expansion.
- It had won territory from Czechoslovakia in 1938–9.
- Beck, the Polish Foreign Minister, was considered totally untrustworthy.

Hitler's demands of Poland – Danzig and access across the Polish Corridor – were far more reasonable than his demands of Czechoslovakia in 1938. Many historians regard the guarantees as '**blank cheques**' given to a country notorious for its reckless diplomacy. Moreover, in the last resort, the 'cheques' were worthless because there was little that Britain or France could do to support Poland. In the event of war France intended to defend the Maginot Line, not attack Germany. Britain had no large army and no plans to bomb German cities: to do so would simply invite German retaliation.

Support for the Polish guarantee

However, and in defence of Chamberlain's **U-turn** in policy, there was a feeling in political circles in Britain that something had to be seen to be done for foreign and domestic reasons. The Polish guarantee was designed as a clear warning to Hitler. If he continued to push for German expansion, he would face the prospect of a two-front war. Poland was seen as a useful ally, possibly stronger than the USSR, which it had defeated in war in 1920–1, and certainly more reliable.

Moreover, Chamberlain did not see the guarantee as a total commitment to Poland. There was a let-out clause. Britain had guaranteed Polish independence, not its territorial integrity. The guarantee did not mean that Poland did not have to make territorial concessions to Germany. The future of Danzig was still thought to be negotiable. In Chamberlain's mind it was still a question of discovering the right mix of diplomacy and strength to persuade Hitler to negotiate honestly and constructively. The guarantee was intended to display British resolve and to deter Hitler from further aggression.

Unfortunately the guarantee angered, rather than deterred Hitler. He abandoned any thought of accommodation with Poland. At the end of March 1939 he ordered his Chiefs of Staff to prepare for war with Poland by the end of August. He was far from convinced that Britain and France would go to war to defend Poland.

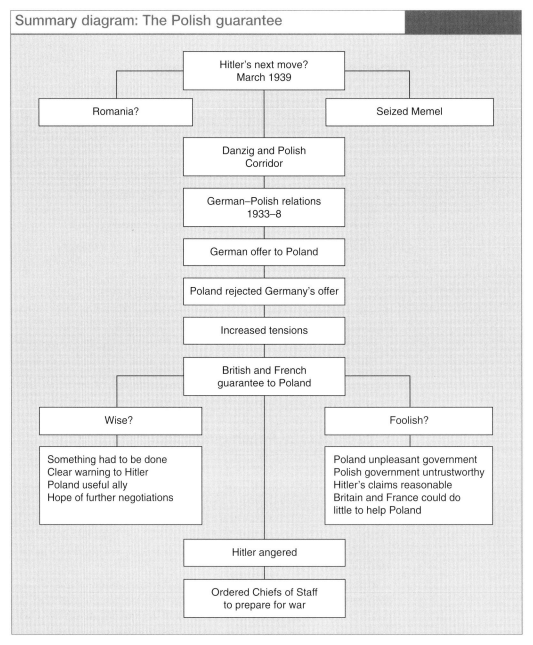

Summary diagram: The Polish guarantee

Key question
Why did Anglo-German relations deteriorate in the spring and summer of 1939?

Key terms

Sphere of influence
An area or state under the control of another, more powerful, state.

Territorial army
Britain's voluntary military force, organised on a regional basis.

Key dates

Britain introduced conscription: April 1939

The Pact of Steel between Germany and Italy: May 1939

4 | The Drift to War

Mussolini's actions

Mussolini was almost as disturbed as Chamberlain by the German occupation of Czechoslovakia. Hitler had left him ignorant of his intentions and this was a blow to the pride of the Italian dictator. Determined not to be outdone by Hitler, Mussolini embarked on his own foreign policy initiative. In April 1939 Italian forces occupied Albania, an Italian satellite in all but name since 1936. He also announced that the Balkans and the eastern Mediterranean should be regarded as being within the Italian **sphere of influence**.

This was a definite breach of the 1938 Anglo-Italian agreement. However, Britain had no wish to drive Mussolini into complete co-operation with Hitler. Chamberlain hoped that the Italian leader might exert a restraining influence on his German counterpart. Nevertheless Mussolini's aggressive words and actions, coming only three weeks after the take-over of Czechoslovakia and two weeks after Memel, seemed to indicate a greater degree of co-operation between Germany and Italy than was actually the case and to pose a further threat to east European stability. Britain and France now issued public guarantees to Greece and Romania in the same terms as those given to Poland. In little more than two weeks Britain and France had undertaken obligations stretching from the Baltic to the Mediterranean.

Hitler was pleased by Mussolini's action. Italy's Balkan ambitions might well preoccupy Britain and France while he settled the Polish question. It was a further bonus when Mussolini, to Hitler's surprise, proposed a close military alliance, which was signed in May in Berlin. The so-called 'Pact of Steel' required each power to help the other unconditionally in the event of war. This closer Italian–German friendship indicated that there was little hope of detaching Mussolini from Hitler as part of the strategy for containing Germany.

The mood in Britain

Most people in Britain now favoured standing firm against the dictators. There were demands for tougher words and actions, including faster rearmament, alliance with Russia, a broadening of the National Government and its inclusion of Winston Churchill, who was seen as a consistently strong opponent of Hitler. Chamberlain was aware of the pressure from his own party, and from the country at large. At the end of March 1939 his government announced the doubling of the **territorial army**. In April conscription was introduced for the first time in peacetime.

Hitler's actions

Hitler used the announcement of the introduction of conscription in Britain to repudiate the Anglo-German Naval Agreement of 1935 (see page 77). He emphasised his desire for friendship with Britain, but he insisted that, just as he did not interfere in British

A cartoon from *Punch*, 5 April 1939. What point is the cartoonist trying to make?

policy in Palestine and elsewhere, so Britain had no right to interfere with German policy in her sphere of influence.

In May 1939 Hitler told his generals he intended to attack Poland 'at the first available opportunity', but that he was still hopeful of detaching Britain and France from Poland and thus averting a general European war. Meanwhile German diplomats worked hard and with some success to secure support from (or improve relations with) a host of countries in Europe, including Sweden, Denmark, Latvia, Estonia, Hungary, Yugoslavia, Romania, Bulgaria and Finland. They also worked, with some but not total success, to bring Japan into the Pact of Steel.

In June, Goebbels, the German Minister of Propaganda, conducted an anti-British campaign, denouncing Britain's encirclement policy and war-mongering. As the summer wore on there was increasing tension over Danzig. The Germans claimed that the British guarantee resulted in Poland refusing reasonable terms. They also accused Poland of launching a reign of terror against the German minority in Poland. These stories, although exaggerated, had a foundation of truth. There were anti-German demonstrations in many Polish cities and the Poles did arrest German nationalists and close down German schools and businesses. Thousands of Germans fled from Poland to Germany.

The Polish government continued to make it clear that it had no intention of giving in to Hitler. Most Poles believed that if they stood firm they could call Hitler's bluff. They had no wish to go the way of Austria and Czechoslovakia and were prepared to fight, if needs be, to maintain their country's independence.

Chamberlain's position

Everything now depended on Hitler. There was little Chamberlain could do beyond stressing Britain's determination to stand by her new commitments. Unfortunately for Chamberlain, in 1939 relations between Britain and Japan declined to a new low. Japan, critical of British economic and moral support for China, imposed a blockade on Tientsin, an important centre of British trade in China. There seemed a possibility of war. Given the situation in Europe, Britain had little alternative but to attempt to reach agreement with Japan, and in the late summer of 1939 relations between the two countries did improve. However, considerable problems remained, not least because Japan was still bent on a policy of expansion.

Chamberlain was less active in foreign policy in the summer of 1939 than at any time since 1937. However, he had not given up all hope of peace or of appeasement. He still thought there was a chance that Hitler would come to see that nothing would be gained by force that might not be gained by negotiation. As late as July 1939 energetic efforts were made to see whether German colonial and economic ambitions could be met without sacrificing the vital interests of the Western powers. Chamberlain was appalled at the prospect of war. Even so, Britain and France spent much of the summer preparing mobilisation and evacuation plans and co-ordinating their military preparations. It was evident to most people, including Chamberlain, that Britain might well be drawn into war over Poland.

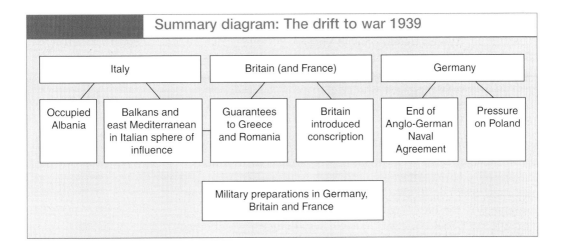

Summary diagram: The drift to war 1939

Italy		Britain (and France)		Germany	
Occupied Albania	Balkans and east Mediterranean in Italian sphere of influence	Guarantees to Greece and Romania	Britain introduced conscription	End of Anglo-German Naval Agreement	Pressure on Poland

Military preparations in Germany, Britain and France

5 | Anglo-Soviet Relations

A big question still remained: how could Britain and France actually help Poland if Germany attacked? French plans were simply to mobilise behind their Maginot Line defences. It would take Britain months, indeed years, to mobilise fully. Only the USSR could offer Poland immediate military help. Most French and many British politicians, especially those on the left, thought the only sensible course of action was to forge an alliance with the USSR.

Key question
Why did Britain fail to reach agreement with the USSR?

The Nazi–Soviet Pact: August 1939

Key date

Profile: Stalin 1879–1953

1879	– Born Joseph Djugashvili (Stalin was a pseudonym meaning 'man of steel') in Georgia; his father was a cobbler; his mother, a deeply religious woman, made great sacrifices to ensure he had a good education
1894	– Entered a theological college but soon became more interested in revolutionary ideas than in joining the priesthood
1904	– Joined the Bolsheviks
1905–17	– Rose gradually in the Bolshevik Party as a result of his hard work and willingness to participate in raids to seize money for the Bolshevik cause
1917	– After the Bolshevik Revolution became Commissar for Nationalities
1918–21	– Organised the Caucasus region for the Bolsheviks in the Civil War
1922	– Became General Secretary of the Communist Party
1924–7	– Power struggle in the USSR after Lenin's death: Stalin won
1928	– Supported first Five Year Plan, hoping to modernise the USSR
1929	– Supported collectivisation of farms in the USSR: as a result millions of people died of famine or were sent to Siberia
1932	– His wife committed suicide, blaming her husband for the misery he had brought to the USSR
1936–9	– Ordered the Great Purge: millions of potential opponents were killed or sent to Siberia
1939	– Agreed to Nazi–Soviet Pact
1941	– Operation Barbarossa: Hitler invaded the USSR
1945	– Victory in Second World War; extended Soviet influence into eastern Europe
1947	– Start of Cold War with the USA
1953	– Died

Stalin was one of the most ruthless and brutal dictators of the twentieth century. In 1939 he had a far worse record of mass murder than Hitler. However, in the event of a German attack, only the USSR could offer Poland immediate military help. In consequence, the only sensible course of action seemed to be to ally with the USSR. Was an Anglo-Soviet alliance a possibility?

The British Prime Minister mistrusted Stalin. In March 1939 Chamberlain declared:

I must confess to the most profound distrust of Russia. I have no belief in her ability to maintain an effective offensive, even if she wanted to. And I distrust her motives, which seem to me to have little connection with our ideas of liberty and to be concerned only with getting everyone else by the ears.

Much criticism has been levelled at Chamberlain for his failure to secure a Russian alliance. Certainly he had little enthusiasm for it. But such an alliance was probably out of reach of even the most determined Western statesman. Stalin's own thinking in 1939 remains a matter of guesswork. It does seem, however, that he had no wish to ally with the Western powers. The only thing Britain and France had to offer Stalin was the prospect of immediate war, in which the USSR would do most of the fighting. Instead in August 1939 he preferred to do a deal with his arch-enemy, Adolf Hitler. This deal had short-term advantages. In the long term, however, it was to prove a catastrophe for Europe in general and for the USSR in particular. Hitler's attack on the USSR in June 1941 was to result in the death of over 25 million Soviet citizens.

Anglo-Soviet relations 1931–8

For most of the 1920s and 1930s British governments, dominated by the Conservative Party, had shown no wish to reach an agreement, or even establish much contact, with the USSR. Both as a state and as the centre of an international revolutionary movement, the USSR was seen as hostile and dangerous to traditional British values and interests. Indeed many Conservatives considered communism a more serious threat than fascism, and regarded Nazi Germany as a useful bulwark against the threat of Soviet expansion.

However, in 1934–5 there was the prospect of some improvement in Anglo-Soviet relations. Faced with the threat of Hitler, the USSR abandoned its opposition to the League of Nations and became an enthusiastic supporter of the principle of collective security. In 1935 it signed defence pacts with France and Czechoslovakia and suggested high-level talks between Soviet and British diplomats. However, the USSR failed to weld a powerful alliance capable of deterring or defeating Nazi aggression. After 1935 neither the French nor the Russian governments made any real efforts to strengthen the defence pact. The USSR had its own internal problems, while France had no wish to anger Britain, Italy and Poland, all of whom disapproved of the Franco-Soviet agreement.

The British government continued to oppose any alliance with the USSR. British policy was to isolate Russia and to keep it out of the international arena. Many Conservatives were angered by the fact that Russia gave support to the Republicans in the Spanish Civil War (see page 88), and some preferred a compromise deal with Germany to co-operation with the USSR. Both Baldwin and Chamberlain suspected that the real aim of Soviet policy was to embroil Britain and France in a war against Germany and Italy, a war from which the USSR was likely to reap the most benefit.

Little effort had been made to secure Soviet co-operation in 1938. The USSR's appeal for an international conference immediately after the *Anschluss* was dismissed as premature by the British Foreign Office and was not even discussed by the Cabinet. Soviet approaches to Britain and France during the Czechoslovakian crisis were ignored. Stalin was not invited to attend the Munich conference.

Chamberlain's policy in 1939

In 1939 Chamberlain still had no desire to ally with the USSR. He distrusted Stalin and feared and hated the Soviet state and system. In Chamberlain's view, there were many good reasons for not allying with the USSR. He believed that a policy of 'encirclement' of Germany, as in 1914, could be counterproductive. It might lead to, rather than prevent, war. British intelligence reported that, after Stalin's purges, Soviet forces were of little military value. Eighty per cent of all Soviet senior army officers had been killed or imprisoned. It was also likely that a Soviet agreement might alienate those east European countries that Britain was trying to win over. These states had no wish to reach agreement with the USSR, particularly if that agreement involved Soviet troops occupying their soil. They feared, with some justification, that once Soviet troops were there, it would be difficult to remove them. There was the added risk that an Anglo-Russian alliance might drive Spain and Japan into the arms of Hitler.

British public opinion

Chamberlain was not alone in viewing Stalin with suspicion. F.A. Voight, foreign correspondent for the *Manchester Guardian*, summed up the situation in March 1939:

> We ought, I think, to be critical about Russia. We need her and it isn't the time for polemics against her. But we must not, in my opinion, refer to her as a democracy – she is more tyrannically governed than even Germany is. The number of people done to death in Germany runs into thousands – in Russia tens of thousands. Altogether, the terror in Russia is such that persons living even under the Nazi terror could hardly conceive of such a thing. But we cannot afford to be particular about our allies, though we must, I think, always remain particular about our friends.

In 1939 Stalin certainly had a far worse record of terror and mass murder than Hitler. However, Stalin's terror was concealed, ignored or even justified by many on the left who ideologically preferred communism to fascism. Even those who viewed fascism and communism with equal distaste were more worried by Hitler's Germany than Stalin's Russia.

Therefore, in 1939 Chamberlain found himself at odds with public opinion in Britain. Most people supported some kind of deal with the USSR. This is evident from a number of opinion polls carried out at the time (see Table 6.4).

Table 6.4: British opinion polls 1938–9

If there was a war between Germany and Russia, which side would you rather see win? (December 1938)

- Germany 15%
- Russia 85%
- No opinion 10%

If you had to choose between Fascism and Communism which side would you choose? (January 1939)

- Fascism 26%
- Communism 74%
- No answer 16%

Would you like to see Great Britain and Soviet Russia being more friendly to each other? (March 1939)

- Yes 84%
- No 7%
- No opinion 9%

Are you in favour of a military alliance between Great Britain, France and Russia? (June 1939)

- Yes 84%
- No 9%
- No opinion 7%

Chamberlain was under considerable pressure from France, from the press, from parliament and even from within his Cabinet, to establish closer relations with Russia. Lloyd George, in a speech in the House of Commons in May 1939, reflected the views of many:

> The Polish army is a brave one, but in no way comparable to Germany's. If we are going in without the help of Russia, we are walking into a trap. It is the only country whose armies can get there. If Russia is not being brought into the matter because the Poles feel that they do not want them there, it is for us to declare the conditions, and unless the Poles are prepared to accept the only conditions with which we can successfully help them, the responsibility must be theirs … Without Russia, these three guarantees of help to Poland, Romania and Greece, are the most reckless commitments that any country has ever entered into. It is madness.

Anglo-Soviet negotiations 1939

In late April 1939 Chamberlain finally agreed to negotiations with Russia. He did so without much conviction. He still saw

Hitler and Stalin as much-of-a-muchness and disliked being forced to choose between them. He favoured 'association', not a fully fledged Soviet alliance. His main aims seem to have been to placate opposition at home and to use the possibility of an Anglo-Soviet alliance as a further warning to Hitler.

Soviet policy in 1939 is a subject of great debate, and Stalin's own thinking remains a matter of guesswork. On the surface his position was serious. Hitler was a sworn enemy of Bolshevism and Japan was a threat to the USSR in the east. Therefore, Stalin faced and feared a two-front war. He also feared that Hitler's eastwards expansion was being encouraged by Britain and France. This had never been Chamberlain's policy, although, in the interests of his country, perhaps it should have been. Indeed, from March 1939 Chamberlain, far from deliberately encouraging Hitler to move eastwards, as many on the left then and later charged him with, was actually committed to stopping him.

Chamberlain's policy gave Stalin some room for manoeuvre. He could afford to press for favourable terms from the British and French governments, and also to throw out feelers to Germany about a possible deal. He made it clear in a speech in March 1939 that dealing with a fascist regime was no more repugnant than dealing with liberal-democratic states. He was in a position to keep his options open and see who would make the best offer. Tactically Britain and France were worse off. They had the disadvantage of seeking Soviet support after and not before the guarantees to Poland.

The Anglo-Soviet discussions, starting in late April and continuing throughout the summer, were complex and slow. British negotiators refused Russian proposals, submitted counter-proposals, which were unacceptable to the Russians, and then generally ended up accepting Russia's first proposals. Halifax was invited to Moscow but he declined the invitation. Eden offered to go to Moscow on a special mission but Chamberlain turned down his offer. Chamberlain himself did virtually nothing. He placed little value on the outcome of the negotiations and admitted in private that he would not mind much if they broke down. His main purpose was to warn Hitler of the danger of the USSR, rather than actually to ally with it.

The British–French military mission

A British and French military mission – which travelled by boat and train, rather than plane – finally arrived in Moscow in early August. The British mission was led by Admiral Reginald Aylmer Ranfurly Pluckett-Ernle-Erle-Drax, a man whose name was more impressive than his military importance. The French had instructions to secure the signing of a military convention in the minimum of time. On the other hand, British military representatives had been instructed to go 'very slowly'.

The talks got nowhere. The Western powers were not eager to trust the Soviet general staff with secret military plans and tried to restrict the discussions to general principles rather than precise plans.

The talks finally deadlocked when the Russians asked whether Poland would accept the entry of Soviet troops before the event of a German attack. The Poles, deeply suspicious of Soviet intentions, would not budge on this issue. 'We have no military agreement with the Russians', said Beck. 'We do not wish to have one.' Chamberlain sympathised with Poland, and did not see why the presence of Russian troops in Poland should be necessary or desirable.

The Nazi–Soviet Pact

Key question
Why did Hitler and Stalin sign the Nazi–Soviet Pact?

The Soviet government maintained that it was the attitude of the Western powers to the question of the entry of Russian troops into Poland which convinced them that Britain and France were not in earnest in their negotiations. However, it is equally possible that the military discussions were a shameless deception, that the Soviets simply made a series of demands that they knew Britain and France could not accept, and that Stalin, courted by Germany, had no wish for an alliance with the West.

From 1933 the USSR had occasionally made approaches to Germany suggesting the need for improved relations. The Nazis had rebuffed each of these initiatives. The idea of a Nazi–Soviet agreement made no sense at all in ideological terms. However, in 1939 Hitler realised that a deal with Stalin would very much strengthen his position, at least in the short term. Hitler was confident that a Nazi–Soviet agreement would frighten Britain and France into backing out of their undertakings to Poland. In January 1939, therefore, German diplomats began to make overtures to Russia.

The Russian response was favourable and German–Russian talks began. By mid-August agreement on economic issues had been reached and the Germans proposed that Ribbentrop should visit Moscow to settle political matters. With his planned invasion of Poland less than a week away, Hitler sent a personal message to Stalin asking if Ribbentrop could visit Moscow by 23 August at the latest. Stalin reacted quickly and favourably. Ribbentrop flew to Moscow and on 23 August signed the Nazi–Soviet non-aggression pact. Secret clauses of the pact divided Poland and eastern Europe into spheres of German and Russian influence.

News of the Nazi–Soviet Pact came as a bombshell in London. Britain had received reports of the German–Russian talks, but most experts dismissed as unthinkable the idea that the great ideological enemies could reach agreement.

Was Chamberlain to blame for the Nazi–Soviet Pact?

Much criticism has been levelled at Chamberlain for his failure to secure a Russian alliance. Certainly he had little enthusiasm for the Grand Alliance of Poland, Russia, France and Britain envisaged by Churchill and others. However, such an alliance was probably beyond even the most determined and skilled British statesman. Poland was not interested in a Russian alliance and there is considerable evidence that the Soviets had no wish for an

RENDEZVOUS

'The scum of the earth, I believe?', 'The bloody assassin of the workers, I presume?' (a David Low cartoon). What is the message of the cartoon? What is the significance of the figure on the floor? (David Low, *Evening Standard*, 20 September 1939, Centre for the Study of Cartoons and Caricature, University of Kent.)

alliance with the Western powers. Stalin had no love of Britain or France. The only thing the West had to offer him was the prospect of immediate war, a war in which the USSR would do most of the fighting. On the other hand, Hitler offered peace and territory. It is difficult to see how any British government could have matched the German offer – Soviet supremacy over the Baltic states and eastern Poland. From Stalin's point of view the Nazi–Soviet Pact seemed to best protect Soviet interests, at least in the short term.

The Nazi–Soviet Pact was undoubtedly a decisive event. When Hitler heard news of the signing of the pact over dinner he banged the table in delight and shouted, 'I have them!' He realised that Poland could not now be defended and thought that Britain and France would realise the same. The way was open for the German attack on Poland, planned to start at 4.30am on 26 August.

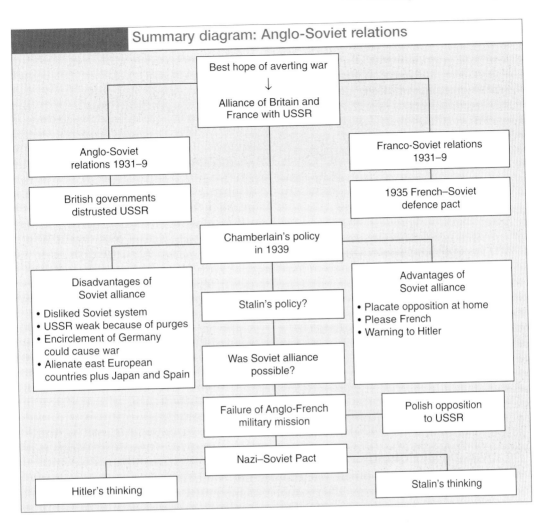

Summary diagram: Anglo-Soviet relations

Best hope of averting war
↓
Alliance of Britain and France with USSR

Anglo-Soviet relations 1931–9

Franco-Soviet relations 1931–9

British governments distrusted USSR

1935 French–Soviet defence pact

Chamberlain's policy in 1939

Disadvantages of Soviet alliance
- Disliked Soviet system
- USSR weak because of purges
- Encirclement of Germany could cause war
- Alienate east European countries plus Japan and Spain

Stalin's policy?

Advantages of Soviet alliance
- Placate opposition at home
- Please French
- Warning to Hitler

Was Soviet alliance possible?

Failure of Anglo-French military mission

Polish opposition to USSR

Nazi–Soviet Pact

Hitler's thinking

Stalin's thinking

6 | The Outbreak of War

Key question
Was war inevitable after the Nazi–Soviet Pact?

Key dates
Germany invaded Poland: 1 September 1939

Britain and France declared war on Germany:
3 September 1939

Key term
War on two fronts
A war in the east (against Poland) and a war in the west (against France and Britain).

Hitler was prepared to gamble on, but still did not expect or want, a **war on two fronts**. He thought that the British and French leaders were 'little worms' who would find a way to wriggle out of their commitments to Poland. However, Chamberlain had no intention of abandoning Poland. The Nazi–Soviet Pact did not unduly worry the British Prime Minister. He believed that Britain, France and Poland were strong enough to deter Hitler. Nor could he have made his intentions much clearer. On 22 August he sent a personal letter to Hitler stating explicitly that Britain would fight if Germany attacked Poland. On 25 August Britain and Poland signed a treaty of alliance. French politicians also made it clear that France would stand firm.

Attempts to prevent war

Hitler, surprised by the Anglo-French determination, was also shaken by Mussolini's announcement that Italy intended to remain neutral, despite the Pact of Steel. The German leader decided to postpone his invasion for five or six days, hoping in the meantime to detach the Western powers from Poland. He made an extraordinary proposal to Britain. If Britain was prepared to give Germany a free hand in Danzig and the Corridor, he would agree to guarantee the British Empire and try to reach agreement on disarmament. The British government saw this overture more as a ploy to divide Britain from France and Poland than as a serious basis for negotiation. Britain confirmed that Poland would agree to negotiate with Germany, but insisted that Britain would only accept a settlement that respected Poland's vital interests. By now Hitler had regained his nerve. He ordered the attack on Poland to begin on 1 September.

There were flurries of desperate last-minute diplomatic activity. Hitler hoped that Britain might have its price for Poland as it had for Czechoslovakia. Chamberlain, like most British and French politicians, hoped for peace. Lines of contact were kept open with Berlin in case Hitler should have a sudden change of heart. Poland was urged to avoid provocation and fresh incidents. On 29 August Hitler demanded that a Polish **plenipotentiary** be sent to Berlin on 30 August to receive the German terms relating to Danzig and the Polish Corridor. Perhaps this proposal was expected to be taken seriously; but perhaps it was intended to drive a wedge between Britain and Poland by demonstrating German reasonableness. Lord Halifax believed that the terms were not unreasonable, but that the German timescale – 24 hours – certainly was. Britain and France put very little pressure on the Polish government, which decided not to comply with the German demands.

The invasion of Poland

On 31 August Mussolini proposed that a conference should meet to try to resolve the Polish crisis. This sounded ominously like a second Munich. However, this time Mussolini's proposal came too late. That same evening Germany claimed that one of its wireless stations near the Polish border had been attacked by Poles. This claim, which was totally fabricated, was used as the excuse for war. At 4.45am on 1 September German troops invaded Poland and German planes bombed Warsaw.

Chamberlain's response

Chamberlain was ready, if necessary, to honour Britain's commitment to Poland but hoped there might be a last-minute reprieve. Mussolini persisted with his conference proposal and Bonnet, the French Foreign Minister, was reasonably enthusiastic. However, Britain insisted that a condition for such a conference was withdrawal of German troops from Poland. If Germany did not suspend hostilities, Britain 'warned' Germany that it would fight. But on 2 September, a day and a half after the German attack, Britain still had not declared war or even sent an ultimatum to Germany. The reason for this delay was almost certainly Chamberlain's wish to keep in step with France. The French were anxious to complete their general mobilisation process before declaring war. However, it seemed to many British politicians as though the Prime Minister was trying to evade his commitments.

On 2 September Chamberlain told the House of Commons that he was still prepared to forget everything that had happened if Germany agreed to withdraw its forces from Poland. He made no mention of an ultimatum to Germany. This did not satisfy many of the Prime Minister's critics. Both Labour and Conservative MPs made clear their opinion that war must be declared at once. At a Cabinet meeting later that evening Chamberlain accepted the inevitable. At 9.00am on 3 September Britain finally delivered an **ultimatum** to Germany. Germany made no reply and at 11.00am Britain declared war. France followed suit and declared war at 5.00pm. Britain's declaration of war automatically brought in India and the colonies. The Dominions were free to decide for themselves, but within one week Australia, New Zealand, South Africa and Canada had all declared war on Germany.

British support for the war

Chamberlain had been forced into a war that he and the British public had always wanted to avoid. However, in September 1939 most people in Britain seem to have accepted the necessity for war. At the end of September a Gallup Poll asked Britons whether they were in favour of 'fighting until Hitlerism was done away with'. The wording of the poll question might have been ambiguous, but there seems little doubt about the resolve of the British public: 89 per cent of those asked said they supported waging war against 'Hitlerism'.

Key term

Ultimatum
A final offer or demand.

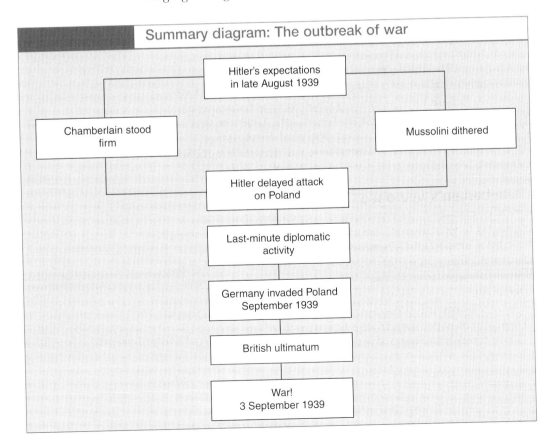

Summary diagram: The outbreak of war

- Hitler's expectations in late August 1939
- Chamberlain stood firm
- Mussolini dithered
- Hitler delayed attack on Poland
- Last-minute diplomatic activity
- Germany invaded Poland September 1939
- British ultimatum
- War! 3 September 1939

7 | Key Debate

To what extent was Chamberlain a 'guilty man'?

The case against Neville Chamberlain

For many years after 1939 Neville Chamberlain was criticised as one of the main 'guilty men' who had failed to stand up to Adolf Hitler. The views of Winston Churchill carried great weight and shaped much historical thinking. Churchill thought the Second World War 'unnecessary' and subtitled his book, *The Gathering Storm*, 'How the English-speaking peoples through their unwisdom, carelessness and good nature allowed the wicked to rearm'. In consequence, Chamberlain has often been depicted as one of the great 'losers' of modern British history – a rather pathetic old man whose policies helped to cause the Second World War. The criticisms of Chamberlain are many, varied and conflicting.

The main criticism of Chamberlain is that he tried to appease Hitler. Many historians think this made little sense. Hitler made no secret of his aim to dominate Europe and the world. He was a ruthless tyrant who was prepared to use war to achieve his ends. In consequence the only correct policy was to stand firm against him at the earliest opportunity. Appeasement simply whetted his appetite and encouraged him to make fresh demands. With each surrender Germany grew stronger and more dangerous.

Some historians blame Chamberlain not for his policy of appeasement, but for his failure to stand by it to the end. They see his policy falling between two stools, with the result that Britain stumbled into a disastrous war against Germany, a war which Britain should have avoided at all costs. Chamberlain is particularly criticised for allying with Poland. Some historians think that Britain had no moral obligation or self-evident interest to fight a major war over Poland. In 1939 the Germans had a good case. Poland was ruled by a right-wing dictatorship. Annexation of Poland would not necessarily have strengthened Germany. It would simply have brought her face to face with Russia.

It has also been argued that Chamberlain should have allowed – even encouraged – Hitler to expand eastwards, and thus ultimately to fight Russia. It is true that Britain and France might have been in danger if Germany had defeated Russia; Hitler could have followed a Russian victory by an attack on the west. But all this is far from certain. Would Hitler have beaten the USSR? And if he had done so, would this have strengthened or weakened Germany? It is possible to claim that Britain had little to lose and much to gain from a German–Russian war.

More recently historian R.A.C. Parker has suggested that Chamberlain did have alternative choices other than to appease or go to war. Parker argues that Chamberlain might have 'tried to build a barrier to Hitler's expansion', through seeking closer ties with France and other European countries, sooner than March 1939.

In the end the main indictment against Chamberlain is that he failed. In September 1939 Britain was forced into war – a war in which she had little to gain and everything to lose. Chamberlain himself admitted that everything he had hoped for and believed in had 'crashed in ruins'.

The case for Neville Chamberlain

Over the past three decades historians have tended to view Chamberlain in a far more sympathetic light. Certainly, he had very little room for manoeuvre. Arguably he pursued clear, rational policies. Most of the charges against him can be answered and much can be said in his defence.

Appeasement was a logical policy to follow both before and after 1937. The policy of avoiding confrontation by negotiation and concession was a deep-rooted British tradition (and remains a fundamental purpose of diplomacy today). Chamberlain saw appeasement not as surrender but as a positive effort to achieve a settlement of all the difficult issues that had plagued Europe since 1919. Like many people in Britain, he felt that Germany had some legitimate grievances. Justice did not become injustice because it was demanded by a dictator.

Moreover, he realised that there was no practical alternative to appeasement. After 1935 Germany could not have been challenged without the real risk of a long and bloody war, a war for which Britain was woefully unprepared and which it might not win. Britain had little to gain from even a successful war: 750,000 British lives had been lost in the First World War. Another conflict might well result in an even greater loss of life. It would also be ruinously expensive and seriously damage Britain's economic position.

Chamberlain seems to have had few illusions about Hitler. He feared his ambition and unpredictability. However, he realised that he was not in a position to get rid of the German leader and thus had little alternative but to work with him. He hoped that active diplomacy could reduce the threat of war.

As it happened, Chamberlain's policies failed and Britain did go to war with Germany. However, the situation might have been worse. Britain and France were firmly allied and stronger than ever before. They had more tanks and troops than Germany and would soon have more planes. Their economic strength was much greater. They also had what seemed like a useful ally in Poland, who they hoped might keep Germany occupied until at least the spring of 1940. In 1939, Hitler was effectively isolated. Both Italy and Japan had misgivings about the direction of German policy and were not prepared (as yet) to risk war with Britain. The British people and the Dominions were united in favour of the war in a way that seemed inconceivable in 1938. Most people felt the time had come to resist German expansion. Every effort had been made to satisfy German grievances, but Hitler had proved that he could not be trusted. Enough was enough. To do nothing was simply to put off the evil hour. The French government and most French people reached the same conclusion.

Chamberlain may not have been totally exonerated by recent historians, but most see him as a helpless rather than a 'guilty' man. He thought of himself as a typical Englishman, upright and honourable, a man of brains and common sense. Perhaps his estimate of himself was not so far wrong. Appeasement seems more sensible now than it did a generation ago, and it was certainly not a policy of shameful cowardice. Like most British, French and US politicians and people, Chamberlain believed that appeasement was the best policy in the circumstances of the time. Its chances of working were good enough to warrant giving it every opportunity. The fact that it failed does not mean that it was not worth attempting.

Most historians would agree that the ambitions of Hitler, and not the mistakes of Chamberlain, are largely responsible for the outbreak of war in 1939. Debate about Hitler's precise aims rages on. However, there seems little doubt that he was committed to expansion eastwards. His ideas of racial superiority and his relentless quest for 'living space' made war likely, especially as he was prepared to gamble and take risks for ever higher stakes. As a result, Europe stumbled from crisis to crisis. This built up an almost irresistible pressure for war by 1939.

For Hitler, war was a historical and racial necessity: the final test. If Britain and France were not prepared to accept German domination of eastern Europe, then he was ready to fight them. There was nothing accidental about Hitler's attack on Poland. He hoped the Western powers would not join in, but he was prepared to take that risk. Given Hitler's aims it seems likely that war with Germany would have come sooner or later whoever had been in power in Britain. Whether Britain would have been better fighting sooner than 1939 – or later – is a debate that will continue.

To the end, Chamberlain could see no alternatives to the policies that he had pursued. In September 1939, in a radio speech to the British people on the outbreak of war, he said, 'You can imagine what a bitter blow it is to me that all my long struggle to win peace has failed. Yet I cannot believe that there is anything more or anything different that I could have done that would have been more successful.' Many historians agree with this verdict.

Some key books in the debate

J. Charmley, *Chamberlain and the Lost Peace* (Hodder and Stoughton, 1984).
F. McDonough, *Neville Chamberlain, Appeasement and the British Road to War* (Manchester University Press, 1998).
R.A.C. Parker, *Chamberlain and Appeasement: British Policy and the Coming of the Second World War* (Macmillan, 1993).
W.R. Rock, *British Appeasement in the 1930s* (Edward Arnold, 1977).

Summary diagram: Neville Chamberlain

The case against Chamberlain	The case for Chamberlain
1. He tried to appease an unappeasable Hitler. Appeasement simply encouraged Hitler to make new demands	1. Appeasement was logical. Germany had legitimate grievances. The only alternative was war (for which Britain was unprepared)
2. Weak and indecisive	2. Strong, successful politician
3. Little diplomatic experience: easily duped	3. Well-informed on foreign matters. Did not trust Hitler or Mussolini
4. Autocratic, pig-headed. Surrounded by 'yes' men and refused to listen to critics, e.g. Churchill and the Labour Party	4. Prepared to change his policies and listen to views different to his own. His critics were not worth listening to: Churchill was a war-monger; the Labour Party (irrationally) favoured war and disarmament
5. Conducted foreign policy on his own, ignoring advice of the Foreign Office, his Cabinet and Parliament	5. Chamberlain's foreign policy was in line with the views of the Foreign Office, his Cabinet and Parliament
6. Munich – a disaster: sacrificed Czechoslovakia; Britain and its allies were better prepared for war in 1938 than 1939	6. Munich – a triumph: averted war; Britain and her allies were better prepared in 1939 than 1938
7. Failed to ensure Britain rearmed	7. Did more than anyone to ensure Britain was ready for war
8. Failed to build a 'Grand Alliance' with the USSR and the USA	8. A 'Grand Alliance' was impossible. The USSR could not be trusted and the USA had no interest in an alliance
9. His policy fell between two stools: • he should not have abandoned appeasement and allied with Poland in 1939 • he should have encouraged Hitler to go eastwards – against Russia	9. He had to stand firm in 1939: • the aim of the Polish alliance was to deter Hitler, not bring about war • if Germany defeated Poland (and Russia) it would dominate Europe and threaten Britain

Conclusion

The diagram tries to simplify the case for and against Chamberlain. Several points, however, need to be made:

- No simple summary can do justice to the debate on Chamberlain and appeasement.
- Arguably the debate has been too polarised between those 'for' and those 'against' Chamberlain. Perhaps Chamberlain was

neither 'guilty' nor 'innocent'. Similarly, perhaps appeasement was neither a totally foolish or an utterly sensible policy.

- It may be that Britain would have been better staying out of war in 1939. Arguably this would have saved British lives, wealth and power – for the greater good of Britain and the world. However, Chamberlain cannot really be blamed for taking Britain into war. In September 1939, given the political situation in Britain, he had little option but to declare war on Germany.
- It is a moot point whether Hitler, assuming he had been victorious in eastern Europe against Poland (a very safe assumption) and then against the USSR (a very unsafe assumption), might – sooner or later – have attacked Britain.
- The historiographical debates look set to continue!

Study Guide: Advanced Level Questions

In the style of AQA

Study the following three sources and answer the questions that follow.

Source A

From: Frank McDonough, Neville Chamberlain, Appeasement and the British Road to War, *published in 1998.*

Chamberlain was not a guilty man for believing peace was preferable to war, nor was he cowardly or stupid, or any more sinister than any of those placed in charge of British foreign policy during the inter-war years. Yet appeasement was a policy which was self-interested and defensive. It was also based on flawed judgements, namely that it could succeed with Hitler and that alliances would not act as a deterrent. Neville Chamberlain's fatal misjudgements were simply the final and most potent symbol of all the errors and miscalculations made by those in charge of British policy during the whole period 1918 to 1939. Perhaps Chamberlain's most fatal error was to believe 'if at first you don't succeed, try, try again'. By trying to get Hitler to turn to peace, he was chasing an unlikely dream.

Source B

From: a letter which Chamberlain wrote to his sister Hilda in July 1939.

It is very difficult to see the way out of Danzig but I don't believe it is impossible to find, provided that we're given a little time and also provided that Hitler doesn't really want a war. I can't help thinking that he is not such a fool as some hysterical people make out and that he would not be sorry to compromise if he could do so without what he would feel to be humiliation. I have got one or two ideas which I am exploring though once again it is difficult to proceed when there are so many ready to cry *nous sommes trahis** at any suggestion of a peaceful solution.
[*We are betrayed.]

Source C

From: A.J.P. Taylor, English History 1914–1945, *published in 1965.*

Chamberlain and his colleagues were not below the average of normal times. But the times were not normal. The freak period in which neither Germany nor Russia counted as a Great Power was at an end. The system of Versailles was in ruins, and British ministers did not know what to put in its place. They would probably have welcomed partnership with a civilized Germany. This was not on offer. They did not believe that alliance with Soviet Russia would bring any improvement on Hitler – rather the contrary. They were faced with unwelcome alternatives and chose neither. But they could not stand still. The stir of British public opinion made them pretend to seek a Soviet alliance. Their own distaste for this made them dream of reconciliation with a reformed Hitler, and this was almost as much a pretence. They drifted helplessly, waiting on events, or rather hoping that there would be none.

(a) **Use Source A and your own knowledge.**
How valid is the interpretation offered by McDonough of Neville Chamberlain's policies between 1937 and 1939? (10 marks)

(b) **Use Source B and your own knowledge.**
How useful is this source for the historian studying Chamberlain's motives for seeking a peaceful solution to the Polish problem in July 1939? (10 marks)

(c) **Use Sources A, B and C and your own knowledge.**
'Chamberlain was entirely to blame for the failure of his appeasement policy'. Assess the validity of this claim. (20 marks)

Exam tips

The cross-references are intended to take you straight to the material that will help you to answer the questions.

1. You should begin in question **(a)** by explaining the interpretation offered. Frank McDonough is critical of both Chamberlain and appeasement. He suggests that Chamberlain's policies were based on the flawed premise that a compromise agreement with Hitler was a possibility. Next, assess that interpretation in the light of your reading of other historians. It may be that McDonough is correct. But what were the alternative policies to appeasement and were those policies any better (pages 151–3)?

2. For question **(b)**, the source is useful for indicating Chamberlain's views with regard to the Polish situation and Hitler in July 1939. He is probably not writing for posterity or trying to convince public opinion. Indeed, he is critical of some of those who seek to influence and shape opinion. The letter may well express his 'gut' views. However, the problem is that Chamberlain is writing to his sister. Is he simply trying to reassure her? Is this a simplistic summary of a very complex diplomatic situation? Is Chamberlain merely expressing his hopes rather than his expectations?

3. For question **(c)**, Sources A and C are both critical of Chamberlain and appeasement, Source A rather more so than Source C. For many decades historians have been critical of Chamberlain's policies, both before Munich (September 1938) and after Munich. There is no doubt that he failed to achieve his main aim: to preserve peace. Was he to blame for this failure? You will clearly need to consider appeasement (pages 97–9) and Chamberlain's policies pre-Munich (pages 101–9). However, much of the essay should focus on Chamberlain's policies in the period between September 1938 and September 1939. What went wrong? Should Chamberlain have given his guarantee to Poland (pages 133–5)? Should he have made more effort to ally with Stalin (pages 140–6)? Was Poland really worth going to war to defend (page 135)? Did Hitler's actions make war inevitable (page 152)? Are you going to condemn Chamberlain in your introduction/conclusion or are you going to sympathise with him? Remember that you should consider the views of different historians on the issue and show whether you feel the weight of evidence supports their claims.

In the style of Edexcel

Why did Britain not go to war with Germany over Czechoslovakia in 1938 but did go to war in defence of Poland in 1939? (60 marks)

Exam tips

The cross-references are intended to take you straight to the material that will help you to answer the question.

In your introduction you might very briefly outline what happened in 1938 with regard to Czechoslovakia and what happened in 1939 over Poland. Make the point very early on that Britain had no wish for war at any stage before 1 September 1939. Great efforts were made by British statesmen to avert war. (Perversely, it may be that these efforts actually helped bring about war.) You might speculate about whether Chamberlain was wrong not to go to war in 1938 and wrong to go to war in 1939. You will need to consider the following issues:

- Neville Chamberlain's aims (pages 97–9).
- The Czech crisis from March-September 1938 (pages 106–9).
- The Munich agreement (pages 110–17).
- Chamberlain's policy from October 1938 to March 1939 (pages 117–19 and 127–33).
- The guarantee to Poland (pages 133–5).
- Attempts to ally with the USSR (pages 140–6).
- The outbreak of war, August–September 1939 (pages 147–8).

As you deal with each issue, you might discuss whether Chamberlain's policy was sensible or unwise. What might he have done differently?

Reach a balanced conclusion which pulls together the main points you have made in the rest of the essay. Was Chamberlain wrong or right not to have gone to war over Czechoslovakia in 1938? Was he right or wrong to have gone to war over Poland in 1939? Was he a 'Guilty Man' or just an unlucky man?

In the style of OCR

Study the following four Passages A, B, C and D, about the British policies in March 1939 in response to the German threat facing the independent states of eastern Europe, and answer the questions that follow.

Passage A

From: a letter from Neville Chamberlain to his sister, 26 March 1939, in which he reflects on the great difficulty of preventing German penetration into central and eastern European countries.

There is always the possibility that Germany will act more cunningly and that instead of invasion we shall be faced with new 'commercial agreements' which in effect put both Poland and Romania at her mercy. I must confess that when small states won't face up to this sort of penetration, even when backed by us, I see nothing for us to do unless we are prepared to hand Germany an ultimatum. We are not strong enough ourselves, however, and we cannot command sufficient strength elsewhere to threaten Germany with an overwhelming force. Our ultimatum would therefore mean war and I would rather resign than be responsible for presenting it. We shall just have to go on re-arming and collecting what help we can from outside in the hope that something will happen to break the spell, either Hitler's death or Hitler's realisation that the defence is too strong to make attack feasible.

Passage B

From: A.J.P. Taylor, English History 1914–1945, *published in 1965, a historian who maintains that the Anglo-French guarantee to Poland was more of a gesture than practical strategy.*

On 31 March 1939, Chamberlain wrote an assurance to the Poles in his own hand: if their independence were threatened, 'His Majesty's Government and the French Government would at once lend all the support in their power'. A peacetime alliance with an east European power had no precedent in modern British history. The Polish alliance embedded Britain in east European affairs. Yet the British government had no means of fulfilling their bargain. In practical terms, their promise could only mean that the French, committed without prior consultation, would not desert Poland as they had Czechoslovakia. But Chamberlain and his colleagues were not thinking in practical terms. They wanted some gesture which would incline Hitler towards moderation and keep Poland available for a second front, if needed. They had no intention of supporting Polish obstinacy over Danzig and, indeed, sympathised with Hitler's demands there, which seemed the most justified of all his claims.

Passage C

From: D.C. Watt, How War Came, *published in 1989, a diplomatic historian who argues that Chamberlain misunderstood the terms of the Anglo-French guarantee to Poland, terms which gave the British government no room to manoeuvre in the event of war between Germany and Poland.*

Mr Chamberlain's declaration of guarantee to Poland bore many similarities to the game of chicken. It left no option whatever for the British government. If the Poles took up arms, then Britain fought too. The decision, war or peace, had been voluntarily surrendered by Chamberlain and his cabinet into nervous Polish hands. It was unprecedented. It was also unconstitutional. It is also clear that Chamberlain for once, did not understand what he had done. On April 2, he told his sister that the declaration dealt only with Poland's independence, not maintaining her existing borders. 'And it is we who will judge whether that independence is threatened or not', he wrote. This was clearly a contradiction of the terms of the guarantee, which implicitly left the question of determination to the Polish government. The declaration was intended to deter. The tragedy for Chamberlain's foreign policy was that Hitler could not believe in the firmness of the guarantee until war was declared.

Passage D

From: D. Dutton, Neville Chamberlain, *published in 2001, a historian who argues that the Polish guarantee was not quite the turning point many thought it was.*

If the Polish guarantee indicated that under certain circumstances Britain would take military action, it should also be understood as a deterrent designed to prevent the conditions of war arising in the first place. To this extent it would be wrong to suggest that appeasement – in the sense that Chamberlain always conceived it as a dual policy of deterrence and a quest for a settlement – had now been abandoned. The door to further negotiation remained open. The fact that it was Poland's independence rather than her actual frontiers which was guaranteed may indicate that Chamberlain was prepared to make concessions over the Polish Corridor. On this issue, if it were possible to view the case objectively, Hitler did have a reasonable case.

1. Assess these four passages and your own knowledge, assess the view that the Anglo-French guarantee to Poland did not mark the end of the policy of appeasement. (30 marks)

Source: OCR, June 2003

2. Discuss the reasons why, despite the failure to agree an alliance with the USSR in August 1939, Britain went to war with Germany a few weeks later. (45 marks)

Exam tips

The cross-references are intended to take you straight to the material that will help you to answer the questions.

1. The first thing is to get to grips with what the passages say.
   - Passage A provides evidence of Chamberlain's views of the situation. The date is crucial: Chamberlain is writing to his sister a few days before the Polish guarantee. The passage suggests that Chamberlain was not thinking of a major change of policy.
   - Passage B suggests that the Polish guarantee was essentially a gesture. Chamberlain was still prepared to negotiate, not least with regard to Danzig.
   - Passage C is critical of Chamberlain, implying that he had little idea of what the Polish guarantee meant. The passage stresses that Chamberlain hoped to reach some agreement with Hitler over Danzig.
   - Passage D is adamant that the guarantee was far from a change of direction in British policy.

Thus, all the passages suggest that the guarantee did not really mark the end of appeasement. However, there are subtle differences in their explanations for this view. Using your own knowledge, you will clearly need to define what exactly Chamberlain's policy of appeasement was pre-March 1939 (pages 127–30). Did his policy change afterwards and if so why (pages 130–6)? It is worth pointing out that whatever Chamberlain's hopes of negotiation with Hitler (as mentioned in three of the passages), little actually happened between March and August 1939. Chamberlain's policy does appear to have hardened. (However, it can be said to have hardened before March 1939, page 128.) Make your assessment in the light of what you already know. Do not leave your evaluation to a concluding sentence or two. Try to integrate your assessment of the value of the passages into the body of your answer as you go along. Remember that good answers integrate the passages and your own knowledge together in a thematic answer.

2. Your introduction might stress the fact that Chamberlain had no wish to go to war with Germany in 1939. Yet war broke out in September 1939 when Germany invaded Poland. With hindsight, it is clear that the only country that could have saved Poland was the USSR. Britain and France made joint efforts to reach agreement with Stalin in the summer of 1939. These efforts failed spectacularly in August 1939 when Stalin reached agreement with Hitler. Why did Britain fail to get an agreement with Stalin? Why, despite this failure, did Britain still go to war to defend Poland in September 1939? The rest of the essay will need to focus on the following issues:

- The situation by the start of 1939. Why did Britain consider Hitler a threat (pages 127–32)?
- The British guarantee to Poland. Was this a wise or foolish move (pages 133–6)?
- British and French efforts to reach agreement with the USSR. Why did these efforts fail (pages 140–5)?
- The Nazi–Soviet Pact. To what extent was Chamberlain to blame for this pact (pages 145–6)?
- Attempts to avert war in late August 1939. Was there any realistic way to avoid war (pages 147–8)?
- The outbreak of war. Was there any alternative to war in September 1939 (pages 148–9)?

Your conclusion needs to stress the main points you have made during the course of the essay. You should also evaluate British policy in 1939. Were Chamberlain's actions wise or foolish? His policy clearly failed: he did not want war. To what extent was he to blame for Britain's declaration of war on Germany in September 1939?

Remember that evidence should be used in essay answers to evaluate the historical debate.

7 Interpreting British Foreign Policy 1919–39

> **POINTS TO CONSIDER**
>
> This chapter reconsiders many of the issues raised in
> Chapter 1 and, in particular, assesses the extent to which
> British foreign policy-makers should be held responsible for
> the events that culminated in the outbreak of war in 1939.
> What mistakes did British statesmen make? Who was most
> to blame? Should anyone be blamed? These are questions
> which historians (and politicians) still debate. It is time for
> you to reach your own conclusions about the skill – or
> otherwise – of British statesmen in the inter-war period. The
> chapter examines the following questions:
>
> - How great was Great Britain?
> - What alternative policies might Britain have adopted?
> - Should Britain have gone to war in 1939?
> - Were British politicians 'guilty men'?

1 | Key Debate

A fascinating question to consider is:

> To what extent were British statesmen to blame for the
> outbreak of the Second World War?

Most historians have been critical of the conduct of British
foreign policy in the inter-war period. This is not too surprising.
In 1919 Britain emerged as one of the victors in the First World
War. Yet only 20 years later, it was engaged in a second world war.
By the time this war ended in 1945, Britain was no longer the
great superpower it had appeared to be in 1919. It seems obvious
that British governments and statesmen in the inter-war period
must be held responsible. In March 1938 Winston Churchill said
in the House of Commons:

> … if mortal catastrophe should overtake the British Nation and the
> British Empire, historians a thousand years hence will still be
> baffled by the mystery of our affairs. They will never understand
> how it was that a victorious nation, with everything in hand,
> suffered themselves to be brought low, and to cast away all that
> they had gained by measureless sacrifice and absolute victory –
> gone with the wind!

Now the victors are the vanquished, and those who threw down their arms in the field and sued for an armistice are striding on to world mastery ... .

Many historians have criticised successive governments for some or all of the following reasons:

- for failing to face up to the evil personified by Hitler
- for not rearming sufficiently
- for failing to ally with the USA or the USSR
- for allowing Germany to become a threat to world peace.

The prime ministers of the 1930s – Ramsay MacDonald, Stanley Baldwin and Neville Chamberlain – have been particularly blamed.

However, it is possible to question the extent to which inter-war statesmen in general, and MacDonald, Baldwin and Chamberlain in particular, should be blamed for adopting misguided policies. Several issues are of crucial importance in considering British statesmen's collective or individual culpability, not least:

- To what extent did Britain have the power to be able to influence world events?
- What alternatives were open to Britain, especially in the 1930s?
- Should Britain have gone to war in 1939?

2 | How Great was Great Britain?

In 1939 few doubted that Britain was still a great power. Although Hitler was prepared to risk war against Britain, he hoped until the very end to avert such a conflict. Britain controlled a massive empire, had the world's strongest navy, and was the world's greatest trading nation. Its economy was strong enough to bind all the countries of the Empire to the British imperial system. Both colonies and Dominions relied on British markets for their principal exports, for banking facilities and for investment, and on British manufactured goods.

However, Britain was not as 'great' as some politicians at the time imagined. Britain's power needs to be seen in relation to that of other countries:

- By the 1930s Russia, Germany and France all had far larger and stronger armies that Britain.
- The USA and Japan had powerful navies.
- The USA was economically stronger than Britain.
- Germany produced more coal, iron and steel.
- Although Russia took some time to recover from the Bolshevik Revolution and the Civil War, Stalin's **Five Year Plans** led to a great increase in Russian industrial production.
- The USA, Russia and Germany all had much larger populations.

Key term

Five Year Plans
In the late 1920s Stalin embarked on ambitious efforts to make the USSR a major industrial power. Every industry had a five-year target.

The British Empire

Key question
To what extent did the British Empire contribute to Britain's strength?

The British Empire gave Britain the appearance of being a really great world power. In 1932, at its peak, the Empire covered nearly one-quarter of the earth's land surface and included a quarter of the world's population. However, the Empire was not as strong as many Britons hoped or imagined:

- By 1931 the most developed parts of the Empire – the 'white' Dominions – were effectively independent. This meant that, unlike the position in 1914, in the event of war Britain could no longer take their support for granted. Many Afrikaaner South Africans and French Canadians had no love for Britain. The same was even more true of the southern Irish.
- British control of India was similarly superficial. It very much depended on the Indians themselves, and they were growing increasingly restive. By 1939 the granting of dominion status to India seemed highly likely, if not inevitable.
- Much of the rest of the Empire was underdeveloped. British colonial policy in the inter-war years was essentially one of benevolent neglect.

Key term

Paper tiger
Something that is far less strong than it might appear to be.

Therefore the 'great' British Empire was something of a '**paper tiger**'. Indeed some historians view the over-extended Empire as a strategic liability, rather than a strength. The Empire cost a great deal to administer and defend. It may be that focus on imperial problems meant that Britain paid less attention to problems in Europe.

British economic power

Key question
How strong was Britain economically?

Britain's relative economic decline, evident to many observers from the late nineteenth century, was a major problem. Wealth usually determines power and Britain's declining ability to shape world affairs owed much to a diminution in its relative economic strength. During the inter-war years historians have seen the country suffering from a variety of economic ills. Some have stressed poor management, an inability to exploit new ideas, outdated technology, poor salesmanship and a low rate of investment. Others have stressed overpowerful trade unions, shoddy workmanship and bad labour relations.

It is possible to overstate Britain's economic decline. Preferential trade with the Dominions and the rest of the Empire helped to sustain British industry through the harsh economic climate of the 1930s.

Nevertheless, other countries were overtaking British industrial production and squeezing Britain's share of world trade. In the 1930s Britain started to have a persistent balance of payments deficit, reflecting its weakening competitive position industrially. Throughout the period the country found it difficult to get rid of the intractable problem of unemployment that reached its peak at 3 million in the early 1930s. Britain's economic difficulties reduced its capacity to maintain or increase its armaments.

British defence problems

For hundreds of years Britain had been able to rely on naval power for security. Battleships, however, were no longer sufficient. During the First World War, German submarines, by sinking merchant ships carrying foodstuffs and other raw materials, had threatened to starve Britain into surrender.

More serious still were aircraft developments. Enemy bombers could now leap-frog the English Channel. 'The old frontiers are gone', said Baldwin in 1934. 'When you think of the defence of England you no longer think of the chalk cliffs of Dover; you think of the Rhine'. Britain was no longer safe from attack. The pre-eminent position of London, home for one-fifth of the British population, the centre of government, finance and trade, made it a more significant target than anywhere else in Europe. In 1937 the Chiefs of Staff estimated that there might be 20,000 casualties in London in the first 24 hours of war, rising to 150,000 within one week.

In the event these estimates were way off target: civilian casualties in Britain during the whole of the Second World War from aerial bombing amounted to about 147,000. But Chamberlain was not to know that his military experts had exaggerated the effects of German bombing. In September 1938 Chamberlain told his Cabinet colleagues how he had looked down on London as he flew home from his second visit to Hitler and 'asked himself what degree of protection they could afford to the thousands of homes' spread out below. He concluded 'that we were in no position to justify waging a war today in order to prevent a war hereafter'.

In the 1920s Britain had enjoyed some freedom of manoeuvre to promote its world interests and shore-up its Empire without serious threat to its position. Germany was still recovering from defeat in the First World War. Both the USA and the USSR, for very different reasons, withdrew from international diplomacy. However, in the 1930s Britain was threatened by the growing strength and ambitions of Germany, Italy and Japan. Britain lacked the economic and military resources to meet – unassisted – the challenge of these potential rivals.

Key question
What were Britain's main defence problems?

3 | What Alternative Policies Might Britain Have Adopted?

As early as 1922, the Conservative leader Bonar Law in a letter to *The Times* had declared: 'We cannot act alone as the policeman of the World'. Yet government critics in the 1930s, on both the left and right, demanded that Britain should play a tough world policeman role, taking on aggressors wherever they appeared.

The left thought Britain should do this via the League of Nations, believing that the League would preserve peace without a special effort on anyone's part. Many on the left called for action against Germany, Italy and Japan and yet supported British disarmament. They imagined that moral force and the threat of sanctions would be sufficient to stop Hitler, Mussolini and/or the Japanese militarists.

The right appreciated the importance of force. However, politicians such as Churchill tended to overestimate Britain's strength. Churchill believed that Britain could and should have stopped Hitler and the other aggressors sooner. It is often forgotten that, in all probability, this would not have avoided war. Churchill's war – or wars – would simply have been fought sooner rather than later and it is far from certain that this would have been to Britain's advantage. At least by fighting when it did, ultimately Britain was on the winning side. In 1940–1 Churchill clung to the belief that 'given the tools' Britain could defeat a Germany which by then controlled most of Europe. In fact it was only alliance with the USSR and the USA that ensured that Britain was on the winning side in the Second World War.

British governments throughout the inter-war years were more realistic than their critics. They realised that they could not control events in Germany, Japan or Italy. They were aware of the fragility of British power and the degree to which it rested on appearances rather than on substance. They were aware of the disparity between Britain's world-wide commitments and the capacity to meet them. In the 1930s the Chiefs of Staff stressed repeatedly that Britain was incapable of defying Germany, Italy and Japan simultaneously. Aware of Britain's vulnerability and the fact that it had a vested interest in peace, British statesmen did their best to avoid conflict.

Perhaps British governments should have spent more on armaments. However, as Treasury officials argued, this would have weakened an already strained economy. In their view, economic strength was Britain's fourth arm of defence. Only if Britain was economically strong had it much hope of winning a war against Germany. Public opinion, which preferred government spending on social welfare to defence, was also a limiting factor. British attitudes (before 1939) made it impossible to consider the introduction of conscription. Thus, Britain had no pool of semi-trained reserves that could be quickly made effective in the event of war.

4 | Should Britain Have Gone to War in 1939?

Throughout the inter-war period most governments had attempted to avoid Continental entanglements that might force Britain into war. In particular, most British statesmen accepted that Britain had no great interests in central or eastern Europe. Danzig and the Polish Corridor, in Austen Chamberlain's view, were something 'for which no British government ever will or ever can risk the bones of a British grenadier'.

Neville Chamberlain, Austen's half-brother, held very similar views. Somewhat ironically it was events in central and eastern Europe in 1938–9 that convinced Neville Chamberlain, and most Britons, that Hitler must be stopped. In September 1939 Britain went to war as a result of a quarrel between Germany and Poland over Danzig and the Polish Corridor. Since 1945 most historians have claimed that Britain was right to go to war. The main debate has been whether Britain should have gone to war sooner than 1939.

However, Chamberlain's decisions to guarantee Poland's security in March 1939 and then to declare war on Germany in September 1939 can certainly be criticised. By allying with Poland, Britain broke one of the cardinal tenets of its foreign policy: no commitments in eastern Europe. British military chiefs were not consulted about the wisdom of guaranteeing the security of Poland (as well as Greece and Romania) and no staff talks followed the guarantees. By guaranteeing Poland, the British government had been shocked into doing what Chamberlain had firmly refused to do over Czechoslovakia, namely to leave Britain's decision for peace and war effectively in Hitler's hands. In 1939 Britain went to war, in A.J.P. Taylor's view, for 'that part of the peace settlement which they [British statesmen] had long regarded as least defensible'. Poland – corrupt, elitist and racist – was not a state that any nation could be proud of having to fight to save.

Taylor's views, which are now supported by other historians, are worth serious consideration.

- What exactly had Britain to gain by going to war in 1939?
- How could Britain help Poland?
- Did British assurances of support encourage Poland to take an unreasonable and intransigent attitude to Germany?
- Was Hitler really an immediate threat to Britain?
- Might it not have been to Britain's advantage to encourage Hitler to keep pressing eastwards so that he would come up against the USSR?

5 | Were British Politicians 'Guilty Men'?

According to Winston Churchill when writing about his ancestor, the Duke of Marlborough, Britain invariably threw away the fruits of victory after a successful war. It is possible to levy this charge at British statesmen (collectively and individually) after the First World War, and Churchill, in particular, did so. Nevertheless, it is important to realise the difficult problems British governments and statesmen faced. Most statesmen – Churchill was an exception – realised that another world war, even a successful one, was the most likely way of throwing away the fruits of victory of the First World War.

The much-maligned inter-war policy-makers did their best to avoid war. In the end circumstances – and Hitler – conspired against them and their best was not good enough. However, it is worth remembering that historians today, even with the benefit of hindsight, disagree about the best and wisest course of action. Statesmen at the time had to respond to crises quickly and with little time for calm reflection. Nor did they have access to the range and quality of information available to later historians. In the circumstances British inter-war statesmen inevitably made mistakes. Given the problems they faced, it may be that they deserve some sympathy.

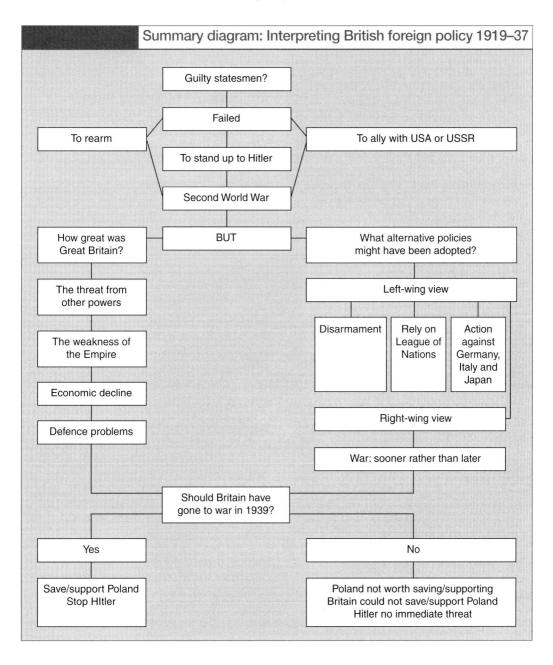

Summary diagram: Interpreting British foreign policy 1919–37

Glossary

Alliance system   Before 1914 Europe had been divided into two armed camps: the Triple Entente (Britain, France and Russia) against the Triple Alliance (Germany, Austria–Hungary and Italy).

Anschluss   The union of Austria and Germany.

Anti-Comintern Pact   A treaty between Germany and Japan (joined by Italy in 1937) in which they declared their common hostility to communism.

Anti-Semitic   Anti-Jewish.

Appeasement   A policy of giving way to hostile demands to avoid war. Primarily associated with British and increasingly also with French foreign policy in the 1930s.

Arbitration   A way of reaching a settlement. This is usually done by submitting a case to a neutral judge or committee to decide the outcome of a dispute.

Armistice   A truce: the suspension of hostilities.

B featured film   In the early twentieth century, cinema-goers usually watched two films: the main feature and a subsidiary film, which was usually shorter, cheaper to make and had secondary billing.

Balance of payments   The difference between a nation's total receipts (in all forms) from foreign countries and its total payments to foreign countries.

Balance of power   British governments had long tried to ensure that no nation was so strong that it could dominate Europe and become a potential threat to Britain.

Banking house of the world   Britain had surplus capital (money) to invest in projects around the world in the nineteenth century.

Big Three   Lloyd George (Britain), Clemenceau (France) and Wilson (USA) dominated the peace-making process. They represented the strongest countries that had defeated the Central Powers.

Blank cheques   Literally a signed cheque in which the sum is not filled in. The recipient can thus fill in the amount. In diplomatic terms, it means complete freedom to act as one thinks best.

Bohemia   A major province of Czechoslovakia.

Bolshevism   The Bolshevik Party seized power in Russia in November 1917. Led by Lenin, the Bolsheviks supported communism. Among its opponents, the word 'Bolshevism' became a derogatory term for communism.

Bomber deterrent   Many believed that no country would risk war because of the terrible effects of aerial bombing on civilian populations.

British Admiralty   The government board that administered the Royal Navy.

British Dominion governments Countries within the British Empire that were more or less self-governing. By 1922 Canada, Australia, New Zealand, South Africa and the Irish Free State all had their own parliaments. They also had seats in the Assembly of the League.

Buffer state   A neutral country lying between two others whose relations are, or may become, strained.

Cabinet   Senior ministers of the British government who meet regularly to discuss policy.

Capital ships Warships of the largest and most heavily armoured class, for example, battleships.

Caretaker government A temporary government. The French political situation was highly unstable. The country was seriously divided between right and left. Coalitions of various parties formed governments but then quickly fell out. The result was weak government.

Central Powers Germany, Austria-Hungary, Turkey and Bulgaria were known as the Central Powers in the First World War.

Colonial war An overseas conflict in defence of Britain's imperial interests. It could be action against insurgents seeking independence or war against a hostile power.

Comintern Communist International (also known as the Third International), founded in March 1919 in Moscow in an effort to co-ordinate the actions of the Communist Parties globally. It was totally dominated by the USSR.

Communism A social theory according to which society should be classless, private property should be abolished, and the means of production and distribution should be collectively owned and controlled. Communism is a more extreme form of socialism. Virtually all communists would describe themselves as socialists. Socialists, however, would not necessarily describe themselves as communists.

Conscription Compulsory enrolment for military service.

Consensus politics A state of affairs where most politicians agree, rather than disagree.

Constitutional monarchy Government where the powers of the monarch are defined and limited.

Demilitarised Not occupied by military forces.

Dominions Countries within the British Empire that had considerable – in some cases almost total – self-rule. They did not necessarily take orders from Britain.

Economic sanctions Refusing to trade with a particular country.

Fascist Party An Italian nationalist, authoritarian, anti-communist movement developed by Mussolini in Italy after 1919. The word fascism is often applied to authoritarian and National Socialist movements in Europe and elsewhere.

Five Year Plans In the late 1920s Stalin embarked on ambitious efforts to make the USSR a major industrial power. Every industry had a five-year target.

Four-Power Conference The conference was to involve Britain, France, Germany and Italy.

Fourteen Points President Wilson's peace programme of Fourteen Points had first been announced in a speech to the US Congress in January 1918.

Franchise for women The right of women to vote.

Free trade The interchange of all commodities without import and export duties.

General Staff The body that administers the British army.

General strike When workers in all industries refuse to work.

General strike of 1926 In May 1926 large numbers of British workers, from a variety of industries, went on strike. This was to support coal miners and was aided by the TUC. In the face of resolute government action, the TUC called-off after nine days.

German militarism The German army had been a major force in Europe since 1870. Its generals exerted great political influence, particularly true during the First World War.

The German problem Since 1871 Germany had been the strongest nation in central Europe with the potential to control the whole of Europe. The First World War was fought in order to contain Germany. The Treaty of Versailles reduced but did not destroy Germany's potential power. The German problem was essentially Germany's power.

Gold Standard   Sterling's value was fixed on the basis of its value in gold, with banks being obliged to exchange notes for gold coin. By coming off the Gold Standard in September 1931 the pound devalued against the US dollar.

Great purges   In the late 1930s Stalin imprisoned or executed millions of people who were suspected of disloyalty. Many of the USSR's chief generals were killed.

Habsburg Empire   Until 1918 the Austro-Hungarian Empire, ruled for centuries by the Habsburg family, controlled large areas of central and eastern Europe.

'Have-not' power   A country that had not benefited from the Versailles peace settlement.

Hegemony   Leadership or predominant power.

Hyper-inflation   A huge increase in the amount of (almost worthless) money in circulation, resulting in a massive increase in prices. In Germany in 1923 an egg cost hundreds of millions of marks.

Imperial preference   Britain tried to ensure than countries within the Empire and Commonwealth traded first and foremost with each other.

Industrial Revolution   The economic and social changes arising out of the replacement of home-based work with manufacturing in factories with power-driven machinery.

International Brigade   A left-wing military force made up of volunteers from a number of different countries.

Isolationist   One who supports avoiding political entanglements with other countries.

Japanese militarists   In the 1930s Japan was controlled by military-dominated governments who wanted to expand Japan's empire.

Jewel in the crown   India was the most highly prized part of the British Empire. It had a huge population and thus tremendous trading potential.

Kaiser Wilhelm II   Wilhelm (or William) II had been Kaiser (or Emperor) of Germany from 1888 to 1918. In November 1918, when it was clear that Germany had lost the First World War, he abdicated and fled to the Netherlands.

League of Nations   A global organisation set up in 1919 to resolve international disputes and to maintain the 1919 peace settlement.

League of Nations Union   A British organisation set up to support the League.

Lebensraum   'Living space'. Hitler hoped to expand Germany's 'living space' in the east, at the expense of Poland and the USSR.

Left   Those who want to change society and who might incline towards socialism or communism.

Luftwaffe   The German air force.

Maginot Line   French defensive fortifications stretching along the German frontier.

Manchukuo   A Japanese-controlled state consisting of most of Manchuria. It had a population of some 30 million. Japan established China's last Emperor Pu Yi as the puppet ruler.

Mandates   The system created in the peace settlement for the supervision of all the colonies of Germany (and Turkey) by the League of Nations.

Manhood suffrage   The right of all men to vote.

Martial law   The suspension of ordinary administration and policing and the imposition of military power.

Monarchists   In terms of Spain, those who supported the return of a Spanish king.

Napoleonic dreams of empire   In the early nineteenth century the French Emperor Napoleon Bonaparte had conquered most of Europe.

National debt   Money borrowed by a government and not yet repaid.

National Governments   Governments that were dominated by the Conservatives but which were supported by some Labour and Liberal MPs.

Nationalist   Favouring or striving for the unity, independence or interests of a nation.

Nazi   Short for National Socialist German Workers Party. It can also mean a supporter of Adolf Hitler.

New Economic Policy (NEP)   In 1922 Lenin backed down from the notion of total communism. His New Economic Policy allowed some private ownership.

New order   Japan wanted a 'new order' for Asia, ending European imperialism, stopping communism and uniting Asians in a great cultural and spiritual alliance free of Western taint.

Newsreels   Short news programmes shown between feature films at cinemas.

Nuremberg rally   Hitler held major annual Nazi Party meetings at Nuremberg in Germany.

Orthodox economics   The usual view of economic experts is that governments should only spend as much money as they receive from taxation.

Ottoman Empire   Ottoman rulers controlled Turkey and a considerable amount of territory in the Middle East.

Paper tiger   Something that is far less strong than it might appear to be.

Passive resistance   Deliberate refusal to co-operate with the authorities. Those who support such action adopt peaceful, not violent, protest.

Peace Ballot   A vote, held at the behest of the League of Nations Union in 1934, to test British support for the League.

Peace settlement   This term comprises all the different peace treaties, including the Treaty of Versailles.

Periodicals   Journals or magazines that are usually published weekly or monthly.

Plebiscite   A vote by the people on one specific issue – like a referendum.

Plenipotentiary   A special ambassador or envoy with full powers to negotiate.

Pogrom   An organised massacre of Jews.

Policy of rapprochement   To renew or improve relations with someone.

Polish Corridor   A small stretch of land, including the city of Danzig, which gave Poland access to the Baltic Sea but cut off East Prussia from the rest of Germany.

President Roosevelt   Franklin Delano Roosevelt had been elected president in 1932 and was re-elected in 1936. The USA had been badly hit by the Depression. Roosevelt's main priority in the 1930s was to get Americans back to work.

Proletarian   The poorest labouring class in society.

Protectorate   A territory administered by another, usually much stronger, state. Consequently, its inhabitants are not citizens of the stronger state.

Putsch   An attempt to seize power, usually by force.

Radar   The use of high-powered radio pulses for locating objects (for example, enemy planes).

RAF   The Royal Air Force, formed in April 1918, was the youngest of Britain's armed services.

Red scare   Words and actions from politicians and the media that suggest that there is a serious communist threat.

Reds   Bolshevik soldiers or supporters.

Reparations   Compensation paid by defeated states to the victors.

Republican government A left-wing government had been elected in Spain in 1936. The government seemed set to introduce a variety of radical reforms, which would reduce the power of the Catholic Church, big business and great landowners.

Revisionist Keen to change or overthrow the status quo.

Rhineland The part of Germany to the west of the River Rhine. According to the Treaty of Versailles, it was to be permanently demilitarised.

Rhineland separatist movement The French government hoped that German people living west of the River Rhine might split from Germany and form an independent state.

Right Those who are inclined towards conservatism or who are strongly nationalist.

Rome–Berlin Axis A term first used by Mussolini in November 1936 to describe Italy's relationship with Germany. He envisaged European affairs being determined by, or revolving around, Italy and Germany.

Satellite A country that is subordinate to another.

Scapa Flow A major British naval base in the Orkney Islands.

Secret diplomacy Negotiations taking place behind closed doors.

Seditious activities Actions against the state which are intended to cause disorder and trouble.

Self-determination The right of people, usually of the same nationality, to set up their own government and rule themselves.

Socialism A social and economic system in which most forms of private property are abolished and the means of production and distribution of wealth are owned by the community as a whole.

Spartakist rising An attempt by communists to seize power in Germany over the winter of 1918–19. The German communists took their name from a slave who led a revolt against the Roman Empire in the first century BC. The slave revolt failed and so did the attempted German revolution.

Sphere of influence An area or state under the control of another, more powerful, state.

Staff talks Discussions held by military leaders.

The Straits Comprising the Bosphorus and the Dardanelles, these form the outlet from the Black Sea to the Mediterranean.

Suez Canal The canal, which ran through Egyptian territory, joined the Mediterranean to the Red Sea. It was controlled by Britain.

Tariffs Import duties.

Territorial army Britain's voluntary military force, organised on a regional basis.

Third Reich Hitler's Germany from 1933 to 1945. (*Reich* meaning Empire.)

Trades Union Congress (or TUC) The main organisation of the British trade union movement. It had considerable influence in 1920, representing over six million workers. Most of its leaders were strongly left wing.

Ultimatum A final offer or demand.

Under-Secretary of State A top civil servant with considerable responsibility for foreign affairs.

USSR In 1922 the Russian, Ukrainian, Byelorussian and Transcaucasian Republics signed a treaty of union and became known as the Union of Soviet Socialist Republics (USSR) or the Soviet Union. The republics kept some local control, but most important decisions were made in Moscow.

U-turn A complete change in direction.

Viceroy of India   The governor of India, acting in the name of the sovereign.

Wall Street Crash   In October 1929 share prices on the New York stock exchange (on Wall Street) collapsed. Many US banks and businesses lost money. This event is often seen as triggering the Great Depression.

War of attrition   A long conflict, in which both sides try to use their resources to wear down the enemy.

War on two fronts   A war in the east (against Poland) and a war in the west (against France and Britain).

Whites   Various Russian opponents of the Bolsheviks.

Workshop of the world   Britain had produced most of the world's industrial goods before 1870.

Index